How to Think about Caring for a Child with Difficult Behaviour

How to Think about Caring for a Child with Difficult Behaviour

A Handbook and Workbook for Adoptive Parents, Foster Parents, Carers and Therapists

Joanna North

FIRST EDITION

Watershed Publications Devon

Dedication

In loving memory of my Mother In Law and friend *Olwen Somerton North* – Sophie's Nanny.

2009 First Edition first published in Great Britain by
Watershed Publications Devon

North, Joanna
How to Think About Caring for a Child with Difficult Behaviour – First Edition
VFV: Family and Relationships
ISBN   978-0-9528713-3-0

Worldwide rights

Published by
Watershed Publications Devon
11 Oakleigh Rd, Exmouth, Devon, EX8 2LN
Tel/Fax 08704051957
Email: admin@watershed-online.com
www.watershed-online.com

Printed and bound in Great Britain

Cover and book design by
Oxygen Creative Services Ltd, Tiverton, Devon
www.oxygencreative.co.uk
email@oxygencreative.co.uk

CONTENTS

Contents

INTRODUCTION

My interest in supporting parents who care for children with difficult behaviour stems from my work as an Ofsted registered Post Adoption Support Agency. I work as a psychotherapist with children who are placed in substitute care when their own parental care has failed them, and I write expert witness reports for the family court on children and their attachment relationships. I meet a lot of adoptive parents, foster carers and substitute carers who are faced with extremely challenging behaviour from children who sometimes overwhelm their normal coping mechanisms and are unsettling to the carer in an extreme way. This workbook, then, is written for you. The information within the workbook is based on research for my Doctorate in Psychotherapy with Middlesex University and the Metanoia Institute. The research is available as a separate document. This workbook is written with the busy carer in mind and intended to give you easy access to the right information.

This workbook is written to help you to think about the child in your care – especially if they have complex behaviour. Routinely we find that parents trying to care for such children are overwhelmed by the state that the child is presenting. This then becomes a problem because the carer becomes distressed about the behaviour of the child. It is impossible for the parent to think clearly and gain control of the situation in a satisfactory way. This handbook is designed to help you to regain your mindfulness towards the child in your care and also to help you to understand more deeply exactly why they are so disturbed.

There are three aims to this workbook. The first is to help you as a carer to continue the task of caring for your child with as much information as possible about that difficult behaviour. The priority is to support you. The second aim is to help you understand more about the behaviour presented by the child and why this occurs. The third aim is to ensure that your own mind is at rest. Research shows that the state of an adult mind has a profound influence on the mind and behaviour of a child. But how do we achieve a calm and mindful posture in the face of chaos?

This work is based on research of current methods in caring for adoptive/foster children and looked after children within the care system. It is intended ultimately to help you to provide a secure base (Bowlby, 1988) from which your child can make gradual changes over a period of time. There is nothing in this handbook that indicates that there will be quick easy changes through technique or intrusive or combative-type behaviours on your part. What we know from research is that change is more likely to occur when an adult can feel secure in themselves about the behaviour they are trying to manage. That secure base is you (Hodges, 2003b)!

We know also from research that substitute parents can start to have all sorts of feelings about caring for the child, such as guilt about their sense of failure that they are not able to make changes or get the child to behave (Lieberman, 2003). Parents can become worried and stressed and angry, especially when a child does not respond to the love that they so freely want to offer. You probably went into fostering or adoption or caring because you had the ideal that you wanted to give a child a good life – and then you find that your own life is being turned upside down. You need to know why this is happening and this handbook should help you with that.

When a child's behaviour is too difficult parents can become overwhelmed to the point that they wish they had not adopted or agreed to care for the child. They may feel indifferent towards that child and not like them very much. These are difficult feelings to manage. Professionals may even indicate that parents are not good enough for the job. This is hurtful and does not help the situation. In this sort of despair we need to know how to think to make a shift in perspective. This handbook should help you to turn that despair into a secure base and a beginning rather than a difficult and bitter end. In fact, the only quick changes we can be assured of are the changes in your own thinking that are going to help the situation.

The research in this handbook is all based on the messages from the work of John Bowlby (1907–1990) who developed an account of childhood disturbance based on the view that children need to feel secure within their close parental relationships. These are known as attachment relationships. When children feel insecure or think that their parents are unreliable, they are likely to display behaviour that demonstrates their fear – i.e. disturbed and even unreasonable behaviour. This handbook gives the practical knowledge that you need to help support your own thinking and your own ability to get that security back for your child. At the back of the handbook you will find all the references you need. Suffice to say for now that the work of John Bowlby provides a secure and reliable theoretical base for thinking about children with extreme behaviour. You may not have time to check out all the theory, but what you simply need are the solutions – now.

You can work through the exercises in this book in your own time or you may want to use it for group learning. It is your choice. You could look at one session a week in a group or you could pack the sessions together in two training days if you were able. You could sit with a friend or colleague or support worker and work through some of the reflective opportunities. However you use this workbook, I hope that it is helpful to you and your journey with the child in your care.

You are not to blame for your child's behavioural disturbance. You are likely to have inherited a behavioural problem in a child because some parenting somewhere has failed to meet their needs. However, the solution to the problem lies in the quality of parenting that the child receives now. The task has fallen to you. I hope this book will help you to feel supported in this challenge.

Joanna North
August 2009

SESSION ONE

Why Is This Happening?

Success is the ability to go from one failure to another with no loss of enthusiasm.

(Winston Churchill)

The child in your care is probably finding it difficult to accept you! That is the beginning of the problem. You may be baffled by this. The child may be controlling and you may feel that your life isn't your own any more. You may feel overwhelmed by confusion and have negative emotions such as anger. You may start to think that you cannot continue to care for this child. These are all normal thoughts and feelings for adoptive parents, foster parents and carers who care for children with difficult behaviour.

The first principle to understand is that you are not to blame for this problem and probably you are not the cause of this problem. You are, however, the solution to the problem. What we know from research is that the most effective way to help children rebalance their behaviour is to put them in the care of parents who are capable and secure in themselves (Hodges, 2003b). Often what happens is that the substitute parents quickly feel out of balance themselves because the child's behaviour is so extreme. Let's try to understand why this happens.

The Causes of Complex Behavioural Difficulties from the Perspective of Attachment Theory

If you are able to understand the cause of the child's disturbed behaviour, you are much more likely to be able to plan to manage that behaviour. The problem that arises is that carers and substitute parents might take the behaviour personally or feel that they are somehow to blame. It may feel very much as if the child has a personal vendetta against them. Where on earth could such awful behaviour come from if it is not deliberate?

The type of behaviour we are trying to deal with may include a combination of some of the following: lying, stealing, not eating, eating too much, cruel behaviour such as hurting animals, constant defiance, controlling everything, soiling, wetting, relentless outbursts including crying for hours, being in a rage for hours, extreme anger, continuous anxiety, lack of fear, lack of self-control, appearing not to be connected to reality.

Attachment relationship

Let's think about what healthy children experience, that makes them happy and co-operative and open to parental control and soothing. The ideas below are, in fact, the theories proposed by John Bowlby in his theory of child development through parental relationships. You will see references to all his studies and work in the Bibliography.

Children who are securely attached have an abiding relationship with their parent and feel they can rely on that parent. They can almost predict their parent's care for them. For example, they know that if they get lost their parent will look for them.

The child lives in confidence with the idea that if their parent is there, they will be safe and the parent will look after them. The child knows that if the going gets tough, their parent will help them out and resolve their problems.

The child will enjoy being close to their parent – physically close as well as emotionally close. Younger children like their parents to be very close indeed and never to be out of their sight. This is perfectly healthy and natural in an attachment relationship. Sometimes we hear of parents who cannot even pop to the bathroom without their child running after them. Older children can allow some space between themselves and their parents. They know they are safe if their parent is in the room next door and that they can call them if needed. Older children can keep the idea that their parent cares for them in their mind, whereas younger children need to see the parent all the time to convince them of this.

The aim of childhood for the child is to keep the parent as close as possible so that their safety needs and need for protection can be met immediately. Once children realise that their parent is always there for them, they are described as secure children. They have what is known as attachment security. The child feels confident that the parent will be sensitive to their needs and they have a sense that the parent is in tune with their needs. If the parent is not (we cannot be in tune all the time), they will feel confident that they can raise the parent's attention until they are in tune. Once they are confident in their parent, they are free to enjoy play and exploration of the world in which they live and will return to that parent when they need them.

Children tend to prefer to be close to one particular figure. This is usually the person who is continuously available the most often. Of course, it does not have to be the mother; it can also be the father if he plays that role in the family. While in the natural world the main attachment figure (also known as the preferred figure) will be the person who gives birth to the baby, in our social world it does not always work out so neatly. If a main carer dies or goes away, the child will form an attachment with the next most clearly available figure because they have to do that to survive.

You will have noticed this preference with your own children, or when you watch or observe the children of close relatives or friends. Despite the fact that children prefer their main attachment figure to be close to them, they do, in fact, accept a small group of people into their lives. So a child will enjoy the affection, care and protection of an aunt or grandmother, uncle or close friend if they are a familiar figure who has earned the child's trust.

We know that if children lose their main attachment figure it is very hard for them indeed. Children will feel a profound sense of emotional pain and loss and they may become depressed and withdrawn as a result. (Bowlby, 1990) You may have noticed this when you have, for example, gone through the process of starting a child at school and seen how on their first day they are afraid without you. This experience and fear of losing a loved one is an instinct that never changes, and it is just the same for an adult who loses their life partner. With this piece of understanding in mind, we begin to see why the children in our care might be distressed. If you are a substitute parent, it is likely that the child in your care has experienced the loss of a close parental figure, which has upset them considerably.

The strange thing is that even if that parental figure might have been neglectful, abusive and even cruel, the child still thinks of that parent as someone they love and want to be close to. This is because their initial primary instinct told them to stay close to that loved one in order to be safe. It is sometimes confusing for substitute parents or carers to see why the children they want to be theirs are still thinking about the previous parent who was not a good or kind parent. The answer is that nature has primed us to belong and to be close to those who care for us. This instinct to belong, even in the face of poor and abusive parenting, remains with us. The fact is that the child for whom you care now may in their heart still be grieving for their lost parent. Here is the first step to understanding why children behave badly and appear to be angry and reject us when we try to give them good care in the early stages of forming a relationship. The solution to his problem is to show the child that we understand their feelings and emotions, however strange or out of place they may be. The journey towards understanding will have begun.

The key to understanding the inner life of a child is to be able to listen to their emotions. This was another key concept proposed by John Bowlby. In the expression of emotion a child makes it clear that they need our presence or our help or support. Some parents find it very hard to listen to and accept the emotions of a child. These are usually parents who may not have had good and prompt responses to their own emotional lives. As a consequence, children may deactivate or play down their real desire to be close and feel protected. They will close down their signals for attention. If you care for a child who has hidden their emotions and deactivated their neediness, you will experience a child who is withdrawn and does not respond. You may find it hard to know what is going on with this child. They are sometimes known as 'dismissing' children because they dismiss the need for adult support , whereas they do in fact need this (Ainsworth, 1978).

Alternatively, children can hyperactivate their need for adult responses. These children are the opposite and they overwork their system in attempts to gain adult attention. Often they do this in completely the wrong way. Inappropriate behaviour can be a way to call for adult attention. It may be negative, but it is still attention and all children love and crave parental attention. It is more important than food. You may therefore be caring for a child who overactivates – i.e. turns up the volume on their calling system and completely exhausts you in the process so that you hope they will go away for five minutes so that you can gather your senses. These children are sometimes known as preoccupied children – they are constantly preoccupied with the need to gain the right attention (Ainsworth, (1978). Their parents may have shown them confusing amounts of attention – sometimes overinvolved and overdependent on their own child and often not attuned to the real needs of the child.

Some children have been subject to abusive experiences of care that are simply abusive. Their parents may have offered them erratic and unpredictable care due to their reliance on substances such as drugs and alcohol. Sometimes their parents may have been frightening and hostile to their children and shocked them. These children will tend to freeze easily if they are frightened or they dissociate – i.e. they appear to be removed from reality and not in the here and now. Equally, these children can be thoroughly disorganised and bizarre in their behaviour and you will find that you struggle to make any sense of what they are saying and doing. There is little 'coherence' to the behaviour they show you because there has been little coherence in the love and care that they have experienced.

I should point out that parents who might have cared for their children in any of the above styles will also have loved their children. They simply will not have understood what it takes to help their children to feel secure by offering some organised parenting. This is where a problem for the child begins to emerge.

Time to think about attachment security

See if you can reflect on the following questions and note down some responses in pencil. You could also talk these questions over with a friend or your partner. You may want to keep a diary of your responses as there are many reflective questions throughout this workbook.

What makes you feel secure and happy in your life?

Who is your main attachment figure now?

Who was your main attachment figure when you were a child?

In order to understand how these children might feel let down by adults and therefore not trust them, can you recall a time in your life when you felt really let down and as if no one cared for you? This may be easier for some than others. We all have very different life experiences. Try to think about how being let down at that time started to feel better. What happened to put that situation right?

If the child you are caring for makes you feel panicky or upset, what is it about their behaviour that makes you feel that way? See if you can describe it in detail. Who are you able to turn to for support?

Keep a diary of the daily behaviours of your child. Take note of the times when the child is most difficult or the times when they are most calm. Keep a note of when the child is most responsive to you or most angry with you. What appears to make that child angry? This diary is the beginning of understanding in detail what is happening for your child. It will also help you to understand what is happening to you in relation to that child. The diary has to consist of only a few words each day to jog your memory. You can then discuss your findings with an appropriate adult or professional and start to notice patterns of behaviour that emerge.

Conclusion

In this session you have been introduced to the key concepts of Attachment Theory as proposed by John Bowlby. This is with the intention of understanding a little more of why children start to display difficult behavioural tendencies. You have also been invited to reflect on your own attachment figures and your own sense of security. While this might not make too much sense now, we will build on this information throughout this workbook. By the end, you will be able to state clearly why it is important for you to think about your own attachment experience. Don't forget – we all have attachment experience. None of us are exempt.

SESSION TWO

How has parenting failed the child in your care?

Why does that affect you now?

Controlling Children defend themselves from the mind of their carer and thereby miss out when they meet with the mindfulness of a new carer and a range of interactions and developmental experiences.

(Howe, 2003)

We have discussed the idea that the child in your care may be suffering from a loss of a primary attachment figure and grieving for that person. This in itself may prevent them from accepting your love and care, and they need support and help with getting over this. This can be achieved by your simple acceptance of this idea and showing them that you understand that children experience these feelings. The child can then begin to share their loss with you. This will take time. You can share this experience together.

What other memories could the child be carrying that burdens their heart? What they also carry with them is their experience of poor parenting. All of our experience is stored in our memory banks at an unconscious level, which means that it is not in our immediate mind. However, memories can be jogged and it is quite possible that small things in your child's new life with you may jog their memory of difficult, painful and rejecting experiences in the past.

It is very likely that your child may not be able to talk about this directly with you as it will not be clear in their mind. Their memories of a parent who has hurt them will also be the memory of someone they feel compelled to continue to love. This muddled thinking emerges in the form of behaviour that is odd and possibly rejecting of you as you are the nearest person to whom they can express their confused and painful experience. Here we have the second piece of understanding whereby we begin to see why the child in your care may be behaving in a difficult way – confusion about the past.

If you understand that such behaviour is actually beyond the control of your child, it may give you that little piece of time in which to find a soothing and understanding response. Instead of feeling anxious or upset, you may begin to feel a sense of understanding so that you are in control of what is happening. What is deeply distressing to substitute parents is they feel that these things run out of their control and there is nothing they can do about it. The starting point is to see this as beyond the child's control.

John Bowlby talked about this set of stored thoughts and experiences as the Internal Working Model of the child, but you can think of it in whichever way you find most comfortable. It could be visualised as the child's internal photograph of their experience of life so far. Even a small child or baby in your care will have this inner photograph of their experience so far. This memory will stay with the child and it will become their 'norm' unless there is someone there to correct it and change the picture with another new picture. In older children this takes more time and you will never completely erase that internal picture, but you can give the child a photograph that they learn to prefer to the old one. In babies and toddlers you are more likely to be able to substitute the picture for one of a new set of experiences, but none of these pictures will ever be completely erased and they won't disappear. We will always have to help the child in our care refer to the new picture and also help them to accept their past. We can never pretend that the past did not happen.

Essentially, what we are talking about is the way in which the child starts to show you about their past through their behaviours. All of those stored memories emerge. The child has expectations in those stored memories that adults are unreliable or, worse still, behave badly or cruelly or abusively, and they expect that same behaviour from you. Suddenly you find yourself like a rabbit caught in the headlights of this child's expectations that you are a bad person too.

> *'I expect you to be abusive and not care about me. What are you doing caring about me?'*

This is the point at which you need to be really self-aware and be able to find the difference between playing into your child's set of expectations about how you should behave (negatively) and how you really want to behave (with love, kindness and generosity, and with calm authority). This is where the real hard work lies and it is why you need to be able to resist the incredible power of being drawn into your child's imagined world where everybody is harmful and rejecting. It can be an enormous psychological struggle not to get pulled off the riverbank into the river of negativity that can emerge. This can be a very subtle process. It is most obvious when you begin to feel negative feelings towards your adoptive child that you know you don't normally feel towards anyone. It is less obvious when you are just feeling stressed and unhappy.

The following are some of the key features of abusive or substandard parenting that you may have to correct and that may be part of the internal picture of your child. Abusive parents may truly love their children but they do not provide good experiences for them. Failures include:

1   Not helping their child with their upset emotions and feelings such as anger, grief, anxiety and stress. They are insensitive to the child's needs and are not in tune with the child on a daily basis. Maltreating parents do not seem to realise that their child has an inner life of thoughts and feelings that need attention. (Howe 2003)

2   Not helping the child to make sense of their life experiences or with solving their little problems in life that then become big problems in later life. For example, they may not help their child with anxiety about going to school or with toileting, or even with their play or general problem-solving. (Howe 2003)

3   Not helping the child to feel safe and secure. This is the most important thing that any parent can do – you may recall from the first session that we are built to be protected by someone more mature than ourselves. It is just not possible for a baby to take care of itself. (Howe 2003)

4   Frightening the child with parental hostility and frightening behaviours. Sometimes the parents are unsettled by the

child's needs and have to stop them from being demanding and so may frighten them. They may also frighten their child by repeating patterns from their own childhood that they do not realise they are doing. (Madigan *et al* 2006)

5   Not repairing breaks in the relationship with the child. So, if something goes wrong and the child gets told off, the parent does not then resolve the matter with the child and 'make friends' again or 'rejoin' the break in the relationship. (Madigan *et al* 2006)

6   Outright negativity and criticism of the child in front of them. (Madigan *et al* 2006)

7   Presenting the child with unpredictable behaviours that frighten them. This often happens when parents have addiction problems such as drugs and alcohol. An example of this would be to invite unruly friends to the house who may be equally frightening and unpredictable. (Madigan *et al* 2006)

8   Ignoring the child's thoughts and feelings.

9   Physical, emotional and sexual abuse.

10   Lack of daily care and neglect such as providing food, clean clothing and clean bedding,

11   Lack of concern and stimulation for the child's development.

12   Withholding love and communication.

13   Scapegoating and blaming the child for parental errors. (Bowlby 1988)

14   Threats of abandonment such as 'I will leave you if...', which are frightening. (Bowlby 1988)

The next exercise is a little challenging, but it is designed to help you understand the inner life of the child in your care, especially if they have been abused. This is the picture that your child is constantly bringing to you in the form of their disturbed behaviour. It is important to remember that your child has no choice but to bring you this picture – it won't go away for them unless someone helps them with it.

You are the most important person in the child's life now and they are compelled to share the picture with you through their behaviour. It may be helpful to remember that we can only offer the child our thoughtful compassion about their behaviour and let them know that we understand why they behave badly at times. This is not an excuse for bad behaviour, but it is an explanation other than a sense that the child is doing this to you on purpose. It is very likely that they are not. Most of all this exercise is designed to show you how the child's behaviour is very likely to be propelled by fear that adults will harm them and not care for them.

TIME TO THINK ABOUT THE FAILURES YOUR CHILD MAY HAVE EXPERIENCED

1   Can you name five experiences that your child has had when in the care of their former parents that may affect them now?

2   Which of these five experiences do you find it hardest to understand or picture in your mind? For example, has your child had experience of starvation or have they been left alone or lived in a house that is filthy or experienced physical violence?

3   See if you can imagine yourself going through any one of those experiences, but don't do this if you are feeling vulnerable or particularly sensitive. Do this some other time. Read about the exercise but don't actually do it. If you do feel you can imagine yourself in any one of those situations, take a note of how you feel inside or what this brings to mind for you. It could be that when your child brings these experiences to you in the form of their internal picture, you don't really see it or understand it (not surprisingly) or, even more, that it upsets you and unsettles you.

4   If you feel unsettled by this exercise, take a moment to think of something nice that is soothing – someone you love who is kind to you or some nice person who makes you feel safe

and happy. The unsettled emotions will soon go away. Well done for exploring the inner world of your child – it's a brave person who ventures into a world that is troubling to them, even if it is just for a few moments. Take a look around the room you are sitting in and name three items in the room (i.e. curtains, clock, television). This is to make sure you are in the here and now.

5   Finally, take a few moments to write out a few words to your child in which you say something soothing to them about their behaviour. See if you can be sure to include the word 'safety' and 'fear' in that little dialogue. Try to use this dialogue frequently in order to help your child at those times of difficulty – for example:

> *'Oh dear, there you go again with one of those difficult pieces of behaviour. I think it is sometimes very hard for you to trust adults and you show me this by your behaviour. See if you can settle down now because you have forgotten that people in this house like to care for children and make them safe. You seem to think that we are going to harm you and it is hard for you to understand that we will not.'*

6   See how many times a day you can include the word 'fear' and 'safety' (in a soothing way) in your daily conversations. Even if you are having a brilliant day with your child, you could say, 'Oh, you're feeling safe and happy today – I'm so glad.'

7   Don't forget that you don't need to know the exact cause of the problem or the exact piece of behaviour that the child might be acting out. You only need to know that it is driven by fear and lack of safety and trust. Your behaviour just needs to address that fearful state and be as firm, soothing, comforting and genuine as possible.

8   Do you have a timeline for your child's life before they met with you? If you don't, this can be most helpful – even if you think you know the history. To lay it out in front of you like a map will give you a map of your child's inner world and may be the key to their current behaviour.

Conclusion

In this session we have looked at how children get to be damaged by parenting that does not meet their needs and discussed the idea that all of the memories of previous parenting are stored in the child's mind. This could be thought of as a photograph of memories that are held by the child. The child in our care will have been showing us this behaviour – and we may not have understood this. It may be very strange and very different from our own internal photograph (or model) of childhood. We cannot ignore the child's previous experience as it will feel to the child that we are ignoring them and their life so far – it is part of them. Yet it may be hard to understand at times and we may even want to run away from observing some of those awful experiences. This chapter takes you through a step by step process to help you watch and wait for clues that help you understand more deeply the child in your care.

SESSION THREE

THE SECURE BASE IS IN YOU – SO WHO ARE YOU? CHECK YOUR VALUES AND ATTITUDES AND SHIFT YOUR LIFE GOALS

HOW CHALLENGING IS THIS JOURNEY?

There is a lot of adjustment to make in your life when you take on a child with a behavioural or emotional problem. In fact, there is a lot of adjustment to make when you become a parent or carer, but there is a need for even more when you are caring for a child with special behavioural needs. Often carers don't consider this and therefore do not give themselves enough credit for the job they are trying to do and easily feel down-hearted and despondent – even depressed.

Daniel Stern has written about the psychological adjustment that an adult goes through when they become a parent (Stern, 1995). He says they have to:

1   Ensure that the child in their care is kept safe and alive.

2   Develop an emotional bond with the new child.

3   Find a new network of people to help support the child and parent.

4   Restructure their identity and sense of self to accommo-date the new child.

In other words, there are major psychological adjustments to be made in ordinary parenting. However, with children who come from abusive and unhappy backgrounds, the new parent or carer has an even greater adjustment to make. Even experienced foster parents will be aware that they have to stretch and adapt themselves to every new child who comes into their home – and every child is different.

The new adoptive parent or carer not only has to adapt and stretch themselves to something very new, but they have to adapt to a new child who is asking twice as much from them as any new baby or new experience or new job. For example, they are having to adapt, grow and develop an emotional bond with a child whose experience of forming a bond is already damaged. That is an extremely difficult thing to ask. It is like working in the dark. You don't know exactly what is wrong and you don't necessarily have the new skills to put it right. You just know it is difficult, exhausting and hard work, and that you are not happy.

Sometimes I work with adoptive parents who find that their network of friends falls away because the friends themselves do not like the behaviour of their new child or children. Even grandparents can disappear when a challenging child appears on their doorstep for babysitting. Sometimes people can be critical when they mean to be helpful and sometimes they can be rejecting. I have heard of parents whose own parents have advised them not to go ahead with adoption or care of the child.

This is an unsatisfactory state of affairs. Not only is a new parent being asked to take care of a difficult child, but they are also finding that their circle of friends – in fact, their whole world – is changing. Your child's school may complain about their naughty behaviour and on top of that you have a child with an inner picture full of fear, frightening events and emotions that you barely understand. On a daily basis the child may challenge your notion of reality and you may even feel afraid yourself. No doubt your whole fantasy of parenthood has been shattered. What you thought would be stories, picnics in the park and an overall picture of supporting a child has changed into a fight whereby the child will not let you care for them.

Parents sometimes start to blame the child, themselves or each other if they are a couple and try to find solutions that will quickly fix the problem. This is not surprising at all, but here is the good news. Many parents eventually find a way to manage and then grow to love the child they care for more and more every day. Usually this is when they have accepted that in the first place the mind (of both child and adults) are made to experience change. Secondly, the brain is infinitely flexible and can adjust to new ways of thinking and being. We can learn new forms of communication and accept the child's photograph of their own life, however difficult it may be to accept that photo.

Some substitute parents or carers may be lucky enough not to have any negative feelings about their situation. Some may feel uneasy or unhappy about their negative feelings. The truth is that if you can answer any questions of uncertainty as truthfully as you can from the bottom of your heart, you will be able to deal with the issues that the child brings up for you.

Whatever you are feeling, the child in your care is likely to have a sense of your attitude towards them. It could be, for example, that you feel you will care for the child but don't really like them. If you can find out why you have these feelings and deal with them with adult support, you are much more likely to create a positive relation-ship with that child. It could be that the child's inner photograph of adults is that they will hate them and that as a result you are responding accordingly. It could be that many people have hated the child in your care. It is perfectly possible to clear up these feelings, but first you have to be aware that they exist, that they are fuelling your thoughts and actions, and that the child in your care is very likely to be aware of them.

The strange paradox of caring for such children is that amid all the difficult and challenging behaviour, there is still the desperate need to belong and that all that difficult behaviour may be a way of try-ing to engage you in an attachment relationship. You need to try to hang on to this piece of information as it could be important in helping you through the baffling behaviour of the child in your care. You may also miss the subtle times when your child is behaving well and trying to form an attachment with you, but you are feeling so awful about their bad behaviour that you don't feel you want to join in. This is very challenging but if you can catch hold of those subtle cues, you will be building the relationship too.

TIME TO THINK ABOUT YOUR VALUES AND ATTITUDES

First, who do you think you are and exactly how have your dreams about parenting been shattered by caring for a child with extreme behavioural difficulty? Let's get down to the bottom line of your feelings. You can truly build a secure picture when you can deal with the bottom line of your real emotions and feelings. Here are some questions to help you reflect on this. You could keep your own private record of your responses so that you can look at them again in a year's time and see how your thinking has changed. This can be private material just for you or it can be a task you may want to share with a confidant, partner or friend. You may want to ensure that the child you care for does not see this information – this is adult work.

1   What are the things that you value most in life? Your values will support your attitudes. The following questions will help you to explore your inner self, thoughts and feelings:

a)   Who are the five (or more) people who you love the most in your life?

b)   Name five behaviours that you most like to see in people – i.e. smart, clean etc.

c)   Name five expectations that you have about the way people treat you.

d)   Name five things that you really disapprove of in people – i.e. being scruffy, swearing.

e)   Name two feelings that you like the most.

f)   Name two feelings that you like the least.

g)   What behaviours do you see in people that are likely to make you angry?

h)   What behaviours do you see in people that are likely to make you happy?

i)   What qualities would your ideal friend have?

2   How many of these values are challenged by the child in your care? This will help you to think about areas of potential conflict. For example, if you value a neat and clean environment, you will be deeply affected by a child who is dirty. If you value hygiene in your house, you will be deeply affected by a child who does not know how to wash.

3   Now let's discover your values on parenting and on childhood.

4   What was your fantasy about caring for a child

     a)   How did you imagine you would feel about looking after a child?

     b)   How did you think it would enhance your life?

5   Now answer the converse.

     a)   What has been your experience of looking after a child?

     b)   How do you actually feel about looking after a child with extreme behavioural difficulties?

     c)   How has it enhanced your life or do you feel it has taken something away?

6   Is there any particular behaviour that makes you really cross or that you find really intolerable? Again, you will find that the child in your care may try to create anger in you because this is what they are used to.

7   Once you have considered any area of vulnerability or any behaviour that might really upset you, it is best to try to guard against this particular situation occurring. For example, if you don't like stealing, then don't leave your best ring out to be stolen and taken to the pawnbrokers. This happened to one parent I spoke to, although she was lucky enough to be able to buy it back (the young person concerned had to pay her back too). However, be prepared to see that area of vulnerability as an opportunity

to challenge and talk with your child about how they might upset adults and how they can expect them to be upset.

Remember the golden rule. Every single event is worthy of attention. Every single event is a snapshot of the child's state of mind. Every single event is an opportunity for repair. All the thoughts in your mind influence the situation and all your thoughts are worthy of your own attention.

8   Can you name five ways in which the child in your care may be trying to gain your attention and make a connection with you –for example, sitting and watching television with you, calling for your attention at night-time, wanting special time with you?

9   Can you capitalise on this subtle behaviour so that eventually it outweighs the old unproductive behaviour?

Conclusion

This section has been an invitation to examine your values, beliefs and attitudes towards the challenging situation of caring for a difficult child. You should have gained the impression that it is perfectly normal to have thoughts that you are struggling with at times. Parenting is a challenging task at the best of times, but a challenging child can really make us think about ourselves and how our core beliefs are being affected. It is only in doing this in more detail that you will begin to understand that some of the values you hold so dear may have to shift or be rebuilt a little. Sometimes we can be so distressed and overwhelmed when a child is difficult that we miss the positive small shifts that they are making towards an attachment relationship. The child really cannot help it if they both fight the attachment with you and at times accept it, but it can be very confusing. Hopefully, you will now understand more clearly why you struggle with this. The aim of this section has been to help you to settle your own stress and realise that it is your thoughts and feelings that will provide the secure base for the child in your care. You also need to be able to provide a secure base for yourself. It won't be a lot to do with what you buy the child or give them or promise them. It is your state of mind that will make the difference. Don't worry if you are struggling with this idea. Move on to the next section and see what happens next.

SESSION FOUR

TAKE A JOURNEY THROUGH YOUR OWN ATTACHMENT HISTORY

WHAT IS YOUR WEAKEST POINT?

This workbook offers you explanations for the difficult behaviour of the child in your care. It also invites you to look more at yourself and the way you think and feel. You may feel curious as to why this is. You may also feel quite cross about this. Why should you cross-examine your own behaviour, thoughts and feelings when you have a child in your care who is simply badly behaved? Such a view would be entirely understandable. This session should help you to understand.

The work of Allan Schore (Schore, 2003) who is a neuroscientist has brought to light some interesting findings with regard to helping human beings change and repair their own behaviour. His findings support the theories proposed by John Bowlby who, some fifty years ago, began to propose that disturbance in children was due to disturbance in the relationship with the primary carer. What this means is that parents are crucial to the development of their child and that the kind of emotional relationship they have with them is crucial to that child's development and relates to all sorts of factors such as self-esteem and the capacity to cope with life and manage emotional states.

Allan Schore calls this a 'mind on mind' experience. What he means by this is that our mind affects the mind of another – for instance, the mind of a parent particularly affects the mind of a child. In fact, what we are looking for in parents is their ability to be 'mindful' of their child's thoughts and feelings and needs – most of the time. You will see from the list in Session Two that it is very likely that the child in your care did not have a mindful parent who took care of their needs. Therefore, the child is very likely to have attempted to survive by meeting their own needs and being in control all the time. This particular behaviour in maltreated children is very difficult for the adults who care for them. It is very wearing to have a controlling child in your care. The first solution is to try to understand why the child is controlling.

1   Children are probably controlling because they are frightened that they will not survive if they do not manage the effects of relationships and the outcome of poor care.

2   They are also controlling because they want to make an attachment relationship and want to feel that they belong, but imagine they have to control the way this is achieved in case they are hurt or abused.

The fact is that we all have different attachment histories. You do not have to have had the perfect attachment relationship with your own parent(s) in order to raise a child who is secure. In fact, some studies have suggested that 51 per cent of any given population may have an insecure attachment.

This does not make you a lesser person in any way. In fact, being insecure can have a highly motivating effect on people's lives and you may be driven to succeed because of some insecurity in yourself. There is nothing wrong in that and in fact my own research diary in completing a piece of therapeutic work with a boy with extreme behavioural difficulty spoke of my own quite severe attachment difficulties in childhood. The only thing I do think is necessary is for parents to be aware of their own attachment style and to be able to see the areas in which they may be vulnerable.

For example, if you have an experience in childhood of being ignored or rejected, you may find it particularly difficult if you are caring for a 'dismissive' child who rejects your care. All that matters about this is that you are able to see your own vulnerability and that you are not reacting in a frightened or upset way to the child's behaviour. Remember, the child cannot help it. Ultimately, we are trying to provide the child with a sense of a secure base. That secure base, as we have already said, is in you and the supportive and reliable care that you are able to offer. If you are shaking internally or afraid of your child, they will soon know it and they will find you unreliable. Don't forget that we are looking at the mind on mind experience as discussed by Allan Schore. If your mind is not secure, you will be unlikely to model or demonstrate security to the child in your care. Over time, it is your demonstration of security and right-mindedness in your own behaviour that will count.

Parenting Across the Generations

Carers need to bear in mind that they can often transmit the bad habits they have experienced in their own childhoods. In fact, research shows that bad habits received and stored in the memory from childhood are likely to be transmitted. You may recall that these memories are stored at an unconscious level but are demonstrated in our behaviour. Of course, you can just as easily transmit good habits. It is quite remarkable how subtle this process is – the kindness in a parental smile may be transmitted in almost exact detail down the generations and will cross at least three generations. Equally, sharpness of the tongue can be transmitted with great accuracy.

Even if you feel you had a secure attachment in childhood, you may recognise that this is not based on perfect parenting. You don't have to be a perfect parent for children to feel secure. You only have to be a mindful parent who is mindful most of the time. The attachment relationship is very forgiving and flexible, and can be stretched. All that matters is how it is repaired and put back into place. Even the kindest and most thoughtful parents will have had their vulnerabilities and times when they have 'lost it' with their children. Parental stress is the most common factor that unravels good parenting.

Therefore, we need to be aware that we will be transmitting our own unconscious attitudes and behaviours, which is why I was motivated to write this workbook for carers and substitute parents. It seemed to me that in attempting to undertake a very difficult and complex job we might be getting in our own way because of our own issues. This, of course, is part of being human, but the research I have done shows that we need to clear these obstacles out of the way as much as possible so that we can create a pathway to help the child in our care whose difficulties will be a multiple of anything that we ourselves can have experienced.

So I am going to invite you to take some time to reflect again on your own experience of parenting and the qualities that you may convey to the child in your care. Whether you had the perfect childhood (which would make this job difficult in its own way) or a ghastly childhood filled with difficulty or even a childhood in which you were abused is not really the point. The point is that you are in charge of your own story of your childhood and that you can think through any difficulties so that you do not repeat the same mistakes too often. Can you make sense of your experiences and speak coherently about your life story?

One of the tests of adult attachment security is not how perfect your childhood was but how coherently you can tell your story. So if you tell the story of a mother who was physically abusive in a way that describes an understanding of that abusiveness and even the reasons why she may have been abusive and what you think about that now, it is more likely that you will not repeat that pattern of behaviour because you will have reflected on and thought through the implications of that behaviour.

TIME TO THINK ABOUT YOUR OWN ATTACHMENT HISTORY

As with all of these reflective opportunities, if you are going through a difficult stage in your life or you feel that reflecting on your own history will unnecessarily upset you or make you feel excessively anxious, then avoid doing this exercise at the present time. Alternatively, do the exercise with a professional who can support you in a thoughtful way or ask your partner or close friend to run through it with you and ask them to think with you about your own history so that you can be fully aware of this.

This is quite a taxing exercise, so I would advise you not to attempt it while you are in the middle of cooking dinner or if your child is going through a particularly challenging phase, or if you have had an upsetting life event from which you are still recovering. You will need at least an hour to complete this exercise. You may want to keep a diary of your responses so that you can look at these later. Please remember that this is not a test of how good your childhood was. It is only an opportunity for you to be clear in your own mind about your own experience so that ultimately it does not get in the way of the challenging task of caring for a child with a challenging past. Don't forget that your responses to these exercises are your own personal matter and it is best that the child in your care does not see your writings.

If you only complete two or three questions, you must always complete question nine, which is designed to bring you back into the here and now in a positive way, especially if this exercise has been taxing or upsetting.

1   Name five things that you really like about yourself – your five best qualities.

2   Is there any aspect of your childhood that helped you to develop these qualities?

3   Name two weaknesses in yourself. Is there any aspect of your childhood that helped you to develop these qualities?

4   What is the best thing you can remember about the ways that your parents treated you? What do you feel you learned from this?

5   What is the worst thing you can remember about the ways your parents treated you? What do you feel you learned from this?

6   Can you recall any difficult aspect from your childhood that you feel you have resolved in adulthood? Can you recall how this was resolved – did you have a realisation or did someone help you? For example, if no one supported you with school work, you may have done well at college in later years. If no one made you feel

cherished as a child, you may have a partner who cherishes you.

7   What were the three most threatening events of your childhood? Who helped you get over these events – who supported you? For example, did you have an extreme illness or accident, or did anyone abuse you in any way? Or have you been abused in adulthood–i.e. domestic violence? Did you get over this with some help or did you resolve the matter for yourself?

8   Was there anyone else in your life, apart from your parents, who offered you a supportive and loving attachment relationship? What was it about this person that helped you?

9   Who is the most supportive person in your life right now? What in your life brings you the most enjoyment and relaxation and security?

Conclusion

Just as water always flows into a vacuum, insecure children tend to find the weakest point in the people who care for them. This session has been an invitation to be ahead in your thinking so that you know your own vulnerabilities and have clarity about them in your mind. In this way you are in charge of yourself and your own responses, and you don't get caught out at times of stress. You don't have to have everything in your mind in order at any one time and you don't have to be a perfect person. Acceptance of ourselves and all that our life has given us is a very powerful factor in our own healing and the healing of others. Ultimately. we have to be able to accept our history and make friends with all aspect of our past. Since this is what the children in our care need to do – we ought to be good at it.

SESSION FIVE
MANAGING YOUR OWN THINKING, STRESS AND EMOTIONS

REFRAMING THE PROBLEM AND REGAINING MINDFULNESS

Perhaps you are beginning to see why in the course of caring for a child with difficult behaviour you may not feel quite yourself – you may feel bewildered, upset or even lost and defeated. It is hardly surprising considering all the varying yet invisible forces that are making demands on your mind, aside from the fact that you have a demanding child on your hands. While you may have thought that you would feel abiding love for any child at any time simply because they are a child, it becomes more of a challenge when that child challenges you in extreme ways.

This session, then, is all about you and how to manage your own emotions and your own internal world that will very likely have been thrown into turmoil as a result of your experiences. The target here is you! What we need to do is something about that turmoil because you will then be more in control of the management of the child in your care and you will be able to think more clearly. Since we have already established that your thinking is what affects your child, this would seem to be an obvious next step. A child in turmoil – we have to help. A child and parent in turmoil together at the same time is a recipe for unhappiness and even more problems. You may be finding parts of your emotions, thinking and self that you did not know you had that are prompted by the child in your care and that actually disturb you. It is possible to reframe the problem and learn to put it right.

It is going to be the way that you talk to yourself about this problem that makes the difference. In the field of cognitive behaviour therapy this is referred to as 'self-talk'. It is the talk that goes on in your head on a minute-by-minute basis about your life. Sometimes we will not even be aware of the thoughts that go through our mind. It could be that if you are stressed, your thoughts about the child in your care are just a tight knot that go round and round your head and make you unhappy. However, it is quite possible to manage these thoughts.

On the issue of 'self-talk', I would point out that it is the single most effective factor in adult mental health (and in fact in child mental health) that we can take control of and deal with. What is going through your head about yourself and your life?

TIME TO THINK ABOUT YOUR THINKING: THE REAL ROUTE TO MINDFULNESS

Sit quietly for a few moments, preferably in a room with no interruption – i.e. telephone, mobile, television, people, etc. Make sure you have a pencil and paper with you and something to lean on. Ask yourself the following question: 'What are the thoughts going through my head in relation to this child?' For example:

He is doing it on purpose.

He is doing it to get at me.

I am a stupid parent.

Everyone thinks I am wrong.

I wish I had never done this.

Everyone hates me now.

Oh, I'm happy for five minutes that won't last.

You can have as many thoughts as you like. Don't hold back. It might be nice to keep a diary of those thoughts and notice how they change over the weeks and months as you monitor your responses to your child and how they develop so that you can come to terms with the changes in you. In a few years, you will be surprised to look back and see how things have gradually changed.

Now we are going to use an NLP (neuro linguistic programming) technique so that we can 'reframe' the problem – or think about it from a different perspective. Neuro linguistic programming is a tool for personal development and therapeutic intervention that has proven to be a very effective technique for millions of people, both in developing their capacity in business and in getting over life problems. It sounds complicated but all that neuro linguistic programming refers to is this 'The way we talk about a problem is the way we think about a problem.' This links with the idea of 'self-talk'.

Now that you have your list, you can add to it on a daily basis but you can now divide it into positive and negative. Pull out your top three worst thoughts that make you feel really bad. Now work with those thoughts and see how they affect you.

How realistic are those thoughts in relation to what you are really trying to do for your child? Now take each thought and write by it at least three counter thoughts, especially using some of the knowledge you have used so far. For example:

> *He is doing it on purpose.* He can't help his behaviour as it is all he knows.
>
> He only has me to turn to.
>
> *Children need adults to help them with difficult emotions.*
>
> His history is so painful and he is acting it out now.
>
> I am a very helpful person.
>
> I am sure I can get my head around this.

Notice how this begins to slightly arrest your despair as you establish the reality of all this turmoil. It is not your fault. You are trying to help. You came into this with the best of intentions and you can plan to get through it with equally good intentions. You will achieve this as soon as you have organised this new behaviour in your mind.

The Journey to Parenting a Troubled Child

You have embarked on a psychological journey and it is quite possible that you were not aware you were doing this. You may have thought you were embarking on a journey that would lead you to happiness and enjoyment and this, of course, is entirely true too. With a troubled child, however, and in fact with any child, you embark on a journey of self- adjustment to the needs of that child. With troubled children this is an extraordinary task for which many people are not prepared at all. It means changes in you.

We are talking about a journey of self-development and change, and it is often the case that we resist change when it first occurs. This is because initially we feel insecure about something very different indeed. Some organisations have a department within their company called 'Change Management' so that they can help their organisation to go through changes. I am not sure if the process of adoption or caring addresses the idea of change management but if it has not, then hopefully you are going to become aware gradually that the changes in you are as important, if not more important, than the changes in your child. It is likely that you will have more psychological flexibility than a child with difficult behaviour.

It may be helpful if we remember some psychological rules about relationships:

So as you go through this process you might like to begin to change your self-talk and soften any negatives that you might be bombarding yourself with. Don't be hard in your thinking towards yourself – allow your thoughts to soften. Remember, you are involved in a task where you have to develop an emotional bond with a child but the child is resisting that bond, which is very hard work. You are also having to restructure your own identity to become a parent and have your values and ideals challenged on a daily basis. As soon as all of this psychological change has settled down in yourself, you will be able to establish a secure psychological basis of understanding for the child in your care. However, while this process is going on, it can be quite uncomfortable and, not surprisingly, many people experience at least moderate levels of distress.

All minds can change.

The brain is infinitely flexible.

Change is possible at any age.

You can always change your mind, your values and beliefs.

It is possible to increase your levels of tolerance – they don't remain static.

Minds can heal.

People can heal.

There are an infinite number of possibilities and solutions.

The Drama of Being a Disturbed Child

One way to start to regulate your own thoughts, feelings and emotions is for you to understand very clearly what is happening in the dynamics between yourself and your child. The trouble with dynamics is that we don't see them and they don't come with labels. We tend to experience them and feel them, and if we misinterpret them we will probably not resolve them. It is very easy, for example, to interpret an angry child as being angry with you. It is more likely from the evidence we have that a child is angry about their life, about loss and separation, and that this anger is propelled by fear. If we can address the underlying issue rather than misinterpret it, we can go some way towards allowing things to settle down.

That is not to say that with a disturbed child you will make one attempt at accurate interpretation and then find you have a solution. What you will find is that you have to make these understandings time and time again – very probably daily and even several times daily until they are resolved and completed in the child's own mind. One way to start to think about your position within the dynamics is to look at the Karpman Drama Triangle.

This is described in the *Oxford Textbook of Psychotherapy* by Giovanni Liottii and is described as follows. We have three points of a triangle.

At each point we have different roles. The perpertrator – the bad guy or the one who does the bad things. The rescuer or the one who does the good things. The victim – the one who experiences the harm from the bad guy.

You may very well start your role as a carer in the role of the rescuer – or the person who is going to make everything OK. As soon as the child in your care starts to show you disturbed behaviour and you start to react, it is very easy for you to take on the role of the perpertrator in which you perform as an angry and unreasonable person (we know you don't mean to). On the other hand, the child you care for enters into your care as a poor victim. As soon as they start to act out in a troubled way that is disturbing you feel you might be the victim of this aggressive child and what became of the nice guy you thought you might have been!

With the help of the Karpman Drama Triangle you can see that you are allocated a role that you did not intend to play. This is the dynamic at work. You really have to consider what happens to you in that role. Here again is the chance to put your diary to good use whereby you can collect information about how you feel at certain times when your child is misbehaving. Could it be that you have become the abusive mother that the child has always had (assuming prior care)? Could it be that you have become an aggressive and angry person that the child has always had, or could it be that you have become a helpless and hopeless person full of despair and depression that the child has always had? There you have it. You are playing a role that you did not want to play.

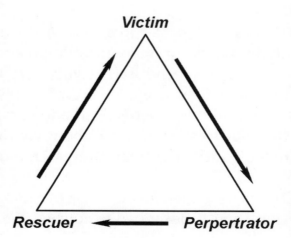

Karpman Triangle
(after Liotti 1999)

TIME TO THINK ABOUT THE ROLES WE PLAY

You need time to yourself for this thinking exercise. Take your thoughts diary or a piece of paper.

Make a list of all the feelings your have when you feel troubled and disturbed by the child in your care. You need ten words. The list is for you to see only. Don't let your child get hold of your workings material as these are adult only thoughts. Don't skimp – write down every thought. For example: 'At times I feel: aggressive, mean, fed up, like I don't care any more, like I could run away, like I wish this child would go away, I can't take any more of this.'

Take a look at your list and consider the words you have written.

Now get a piece of paper and some coloured crayons and, whether or not you think you are an artist or whether you just draw stick people does not matter, draw a picture of that person. Use colour to indicate different moods like anger, fear, despair. Preferably use as big a piece of paper as possible, but even if you only have a piece of writing paper, draw that picture. Enjoy it – have fun.

Now give that person a name. Here are some suggestions:

Cruella de Vil

The Dinosaur Dad

Deadly Demon

The Witch from Hell

The Hag

The Dragon

There could be all sorts of names. Some may be amusing, some may be ordinary. My preferred name, for example, is the Witch from Hell.

Now your dynamic has become something more tangible for you to consider. There may be a little bit of you that really is this person. Try to establish how much of you this person really is. It is more than likely that you will find aspects of yourself in this personality. There may be aspects of yourself that definitely are not this person. You may not identify in any way with the abuser you feel your child wants you to be.

The important aspect of this exercise is that we have externalised the role that your child may have wanted you to play and that you have come to understand that role a little more, and it gives you a foothold into whether or not you feel you actually want to play that role. So when, for example, I feel myself beginning to act like the screaming Witch from Hell, I am likely to recognise this more quickly and am likely to get my 'self-talk' together and have more control over the situation . Here is an example.

Talking Back to the Witch from Hell

Do you really want to play that role right now?

How were you feeling five minutes ago? Did you want to shift into this role?

If I play this role will it help?

If I play this role will it help the child?

Could I talk to my partner/friend about this role instead?

I could keep a record of how many times a day I become this role.

I could have a screaming witch party with my friends rather than act this out when I don't want to.

I actually have a choice about when I do this.

I love that screaming witch for how much effort she makes to help this child.

That witch is so co-operative with this dynamic

And so the conversation with your self starts. However, it is better to have a conversation with the screaming Witch from Hell than to have her exaggerate the problem and support your child's view and self-talk: 'See! The world really is full of screaming witches – I knew it.'

It can be equally difficult to play the opposite role – i.e. the Fairy Godmother or Godfather. You are equally liable to fall from this position with a great crash one day. Sometimes it can occur with couples that one half of the couple can play the negative role and the other half the positive, which seems grossly unfair, especially to the one with the negative role to play. Couples who are caring need to get their heads together and start a dialogue so that these roles can balance out in the dynamic with the child.

Stress

You will be stressed when you take on a difficult child to care for. In fact, you will be stressed by any new role you are asked to take on. With a child it is particularly difficult and stressful because it affects you personally.

There are many ways to combat stress, but first of all you need to understand it – how stress affects you and what stress actually is. Stress is any situation in which you feel overwhelmed and beyond your coping capacity or threatened. You are therefore anxious and go into fight or flight mode and begin to feel panic, which sends chemicals called adrenalin and cortisol into your system. The cortisol increases your blood sugar and speeds up your metabolism. The adrenalin prepares you for a fight or flight response – either way, you are ready for 'action', primed and ready for a day of stress.

A certain a mount of stress is very good for us and could be triggered by everyday events such as being under pressure to complete a deadline or running for a bus or being in an important meeting where we have to make your point or give a presentation. A limited amount of stress in our lives enables us able to cope and increases our capacity to manage stress. So a person giving a presentation after 500 presentations will have learned the skill of managing stress. A person giving a presentation for the first time will think that they may not survive the experience.

What is clear is that constant stress through relentless problems is not actually healthy or good for people. Managing stress is a skill that we can learn. So whether you are very stressed by your situation or just a little stressed, the good news is that there are so many things to do to combat stress.

Some years ago I interviewed parents who cared for difficult children and who were very successful at it, and I asked them for their advice to other carers. All of them told me that they found ways to deal with stress. Some did this through exercise, some did it through a hobby, some did meditation and some did singing. They were pretty impressive people, but anyone who combats and overcomes the things that they fear will be a person worthy of note.

What is not advisable is to attack stress in self-destructive ways. Sadly, this is the easiest thing to do. So a bottle of wine at night, excessive food or falling asleep to cope is not likely to help you in the long term, although it may help in the short term. A well-calculated response means that you are back in control, whereas a maladaptive response means that you are likely to get caught in a cycle of stress and despair. Since that is the one thing that is not going to help, all carers need to watch their stress levels and monitor them on a daily basis. A small change in your habits can make a very big difference to your stress levels.

Time management helps with stress

One of the best ways to introduce stress reduction techniques into your life is to go on a stress management course. Ultimately, however, you must have a plan and be able to timetable changes into your life. There is no doubt that when your life is swamped by the demands and anxieties of a difficult child, the last thing you think of doing is planning time out! However, you must do this.

One of the best and most powerful ways to take control of your life and help you stay in control when you are battling against over-whelming odds is to timetable how you want your day to be. In this way you can manage events as you decide they will arise. You can also make risk assessments of risky times that may defeat you. For example, if you plan Saturday afternoon at the beach in August, you need to plan in the amount of anxiety you will expend wondering if the child in your care will either drown or get lost. On reflection and having taken that risk assessment, you may decide that sunbathing in the garden in August and a picnic in the garden is far less stressful as you can keep your eye on things.

You cannot timetable for everything in life, and skilful and success-ful people are always flexible and able to adapt their plans. That is the point of a plan – you are in charge of it, rather than having acres of time in which the child in your care may feel insecure as they don't know what is happening next. One of my successful adoptive par-ents always had a plan on her wall one week at a time, even during term time. This helped her adoptive child to predict what was hap-pening next and gave him less excuse to be so controlling. The same parent also had a plan for the summer holidays, which were a time for increased anxiety when children are very excited.

Your thinking

We started this session by thinking about 'self-talk'. It is very common for people's thoughts to run riot and be very speedy and irrational when they are under stress. You need to watch for this tendency as it is more than likely to occur at times of extreme stress or when you are upset. You are at your most vulnerable at these times and you don't need any extra opportunities for uncontrolled emotions – your child will be struggling with these enough as it is.

Some things to remember about your thinking that people often do not understand is that it is entirely under your control and you have a choice about what you think. If you understand this basic principle of behaviour, you can truly be in command of yourself and your actions in the future, and you are more likely to help your child also to understand the principle of taking responsibility for their own thoughts and actions. The basic rule of changing behaviour is to be able to connect with the idea that 'all behaviour is a choice'. We must be aware that we have a choice. This again would be a starting point for helping a difficult child to understand that their behaviour is a choice too. You are the model for this.

A psychiatrist who was very adept at understanding this was Albert Ellis who developed a form of therapy called Rational Emotive Behaviour Therapy. Essentially, he could see that panic and stress overworked the fight or flight response of the mind and led to irrational behaviour that was fuelled by stress chemicals. This has sometimes been called 'mind over matter'. This implies that it is our thoughts that lead to our feelings and emotional states. Imagine how we provoke awful feelings when our thoughts constantly run out of control. Ellis suggested that we look at the irrational beliefs that actually lead to our emotional distress. He cleverly pulled out some common irrational beliefs that people hold in their minds and allow to run their lives. For example:

> *I must be liked or accepted by everyone in my life at all times.*
>
> *I must be successful and competent at everything I do.*
>
> *It is awful and terrible when things are not the way I would like them to be.*
>
> *People have no ability to control their negative feelings.*
>
> *I must be in control at all times.*
>
> (Ellis and Harper, 1975)

If you think about it, these thoughts are actually without basis. It is impossible to be accepted by everyone, you cannot be successful at everything, things cannot always be the way you would like them to be, and you do have the ability to control your negative feelings (in fact, much of Ellis' book is taken up with that idea). If you take all the thoughts that run through your head in relation to a difficult child who makes you panic, you will see that they are just that – panic thoughts.

If you begin to understand the principles of this session, you will be on the way to becoming a more effective manager of the child in your care. There may be days when you don't feel a lot of love and affection for a difficult child. This is not as important as continuing to care for them and provide a secure base and be there for them. There will be plenty of time in the future when your child is feeling safe in your care when you will be able to experience the luxury of enjoyment, love and affection in your relationship with them. In the meantime, the thinking in this session is designed to help you over the difficult times so that you feel just about good enough on a daily basis to cope because you are not stressed.

TIME TO THINK ABOUT YOUR NEW STRESS MANAGEMENT PROGRAMME

Back to your diary or note keeping.

The following questions are designed to prompt your thinking with regard to enhancing your own life while you cope with the overwhelming and relentless needs of the child in your care. It is not a good idea for you to become a victim of such difficulty and ensuring that you have quality time in which to relax will make a difference to your state of mind and well being. If you recall, we are looking at 'caregiver state of mind' all the time here – we know that your state of mind makes all the difference.

What are your ten most favourite things to do in life that help you relax?

When did you last do these?

How can you timetable them into your life?

How much time do you get to relax and think?

What helps you to relax and think (dancing, meditation, boxing, cake making, sewing)?

What hobby do you closely identify with?

Does stress affect you mentally, physically, emotionally, or in all ways?

Do you adopt negative strategies to combat stress (drink, food, caffeine, shouting)?

How can you gradually shift these strategies?

Now how can you start to implement these activities in your life? I have put a time management chart in this workbook for your use. I would like you to notice how you change your stress levels by planning your weeks. Plan every week for a month and notice the impact that it has on your sense of self, your state of mind and the child in your care.

It is imperative that you plan in time for yourself. You need at least one session a week but preferably more. You will need to speak with your partner about this so that you can each find time for your selves and find time for your selves as a couple. So you could cover each other for 'time to myself' and you would need support for time as a couple. If you are a single carer – many carers are – you will need to call on your friends or exchange favours with another single carer. Don't be defeated. There are people out there who will help you. One foster carer I spoke with made the simple step of putting a mini trampette in her garage. She found that bouncing for five minutes a day made her more relaxed and stronger. She also put up a hammock in her garage and could lie down quietly for twenty minutes and relax at least once a day. She reports that this makes a big difference to her attitude.

Conclusion

You may wonder when we will get to think more about the child in your care rather than you. We will be moving on in the next session. This session underlies the key concept that it is your own state of mind that will make the difference – however difficult things become with the child in your care. If your mind is still and quiet, it is far more likely that you will find good solutions to difficult problems. If your mind is racing with crazy thoughts, you are less likely to make the right decisions. In this session we have talked about your thoughts and how to manage what is in your mind. We have discussed making small plans to make fundamental changes in your timetable. Don't forget to tell people about the changes. The more people who are on board with your plan, the more likely you are to feel supported. Ultimately, you are the master of your own destiny and the child in your care is learning that competent, safe people can provide them with a secure base so that they can relax and enjoy life rather than act on their unhappy inner world, just as you are showing them. In Session Six we will talk more about forming that relationship.

Week Beginning .... **Name** ....

	Monday	Tuesday	Wednesday	Thursday	Friday	Saturday	Sunday
Wake until 9am							
10am until 11am							
11am until 12 noon							
12 noon until 1pm							
1pm until 2pm							
2pm until 3pm							
3pm until 4pm							
4pm until 5pm							
5pm until 6pm							
6pm until 7pm							
7pm until 8pm							
8pm until 9pm							
9pm until bedtime							

SESSION SIX

WORKING WITH YOUR CHILD
THE JOURNEY FROM SECURE TO INSECURE
HOW TO BUILD AN ALLIANCE AS A STARTING
POINT

This workbook is intended to help you build a picture of why the child in your care will be so challenging. We are also building a picture of your responses to the child in your care to help you to rethink and replan, and gradually build that all-important secure base with and for your child. Essentially, we have been talking about the idea that you and the child in your care may have different realities. Ultimately, our goal is a shared sense of the world and relationships. Our task is to help the child feel secure so that they can get on with their life and not continue acting out (which defeats their happiness).

Your reality may be based on secure parenting in which your parents supported you and helped you to feel good about coping with life. Alternatively, your reality may be based on insecure parenting in which you were not supported enough, but you have learned your security through the support of others or just by the process of life and watching others. Many people do this and no way is better than the other. However, the child in your care will not be in your care because they are secure. Children who have been put through the care system are not subject to this experience because they have a secure upbringing. In fact, they are not subject to care proceedings because they have had an insecure upbringing. They are subject to proceedings because their whole experience has moved on a level, to an abusive and neglectful upbringing. This scars a child very badly. Those scars are brought into the new relationship with new carers and, as we have already established, they are easily reopened.

It is highly likely, therefore, that unless you have recovered from an abusive upbringing yourself (if you have, you are marvellous and will probably understand this process) your inner realities will be very different indeed. In this workbook I am trying to help you to bridge the gap between your own internal reality of relationship and that of your child, which is probably very baffling and strange to you. For example, children who have been abused and hurt badly often have to defend themselves from any kind of relationship at all with anyone and find it safer to live in their own 'unattached' world run by their own rules, whereas people who have had secure attachments find that they enjoy relationships with others and have a sense of connectedness and support – they believe that relationships will not fail them. The child in your care probably believes that any relationship will fail them.

With that in mind, it is not surprising that a new adoptive parent or supportive carer, full of love, affection, fun and believing in life, is a bit of a shock to a child who has decided that relationships are a waste of time. This is the discrepancy that we are trying to deal with in this session. Believe it or not , your initial desire to be kind, loving and thoughtful may be quite frightening to the child you are about to love and care for. So how do we help a child with that fear and how do we help you with dealing with it?

From trawling through current literature and understanding about these types of challenge with severely damaged children, it would appear that the most helpful stance to take is that of forming and building an alliance with your child rather than trying to form an affectionate relationship that everyone else can take for granted. So the basis of the relationship building may need to be different. Hopefully, we have established the idea that this is a process over a period of time and that we must really try to avoid thinking that this is a single event in which a child gets cured. This is a fundamental rule that will help you not to be disappointed when you find that you have to repeat yourself time and time again, so that the child in your care can get used to new patterns of experience and bed them down in their memory banks. Children who have been abused and harmed often find it hard to think straight – their capacity to think things through becomes muddled very easily and it will take many many hours to establish new thoughts.

Parents have to become very skilled at interceding in their child's life with them and for them. It has to be accepted that the child is going to find it hard to change their own behaviour, which may be upsetting and annoying but is probably beyond their control. The ground rules of the relationship are going to be different. It is best to think of yourself as building an alliance initially rather than entering into a relationship. This means that you should not overcrowd the child with your love and good intentions (which may be a threat to the child), but at the same time you should not ignore them to get on with life on their own (and they may very likely give the impression that they would like to do this). It is an incredible skill to achieve this fine balance and I hope that some of the ideas in this session will help you to do this.

In Session Five I discussed the secure base that you create in yourself – your sense of an emotionally balanced life so that the child in your care can rely on you (even if you don't feel reliable at times – and you won't feel that way all the time). Or at least perhaps they can rely on your ability to rebalance yourself when things become difficult. From that secure and mindful base, it is easier to start observing the special needs of the child in your care, and seeing what really helps them, rather than what you think they need based on the assumption that they are an ordinary child.

Don't get too close too soon

It is sad when a wonderfully well-meaning carer offers their heart to a child only to see them severely and often aggressively pushed away. Trying to get too close too soon is often the first mistake that a new carer will make. It is a bit like offering a feast to someone who has starved in the desert – it would make them very sick to eat all that rich food. I have met some wonderful adoptive parents who are full of love and who pile their new child's life high with all the normal things of childhood: outings, games, toys, treats, films, conversations, parties, etc. Sometimes I wonder how secure children cope with so many treats in their lives – but that is the subject of another book. I once watched a newly adoptive boy behave as if he was drunk – he was completely dislodged by having so many treats in his life. The parents were eventually confounded as he seemed so ungrateful and none of the goodies helped his behaviour at all, and the toys were frequently broken and abused as a demonstration of how he really felt about his life.

So another rule that must be established is that too much too soon is too awful for the child in your care. That does not mean that you should behave in a depriving way. It just means that you should be mindful that too much at once may make your child 'sick' – like the person from the desert who is offered a feast after suffering from starvation. It may make your child feel intensely unhappy as they realise how badly deprived they feel inside. Since they cannot explain that feeling, they may well take this out on you.

Getting skilled at understanding states of mind

Parents and carers have to be very skilled at understanding the child's different states of mind. They have to crack the code of meaning, decipher the communication and make sense of their behaviour. This may also take plenty of time and carers must not be upset with themselves for not getting it right first time. As a psychotherapist working with many deprived and unhappy children, I note that some-times it takes me years to really understand a child and how they work. Very often all I can do is help a parent to understand so that we form an alliance together of support and understanding.

Let's take, for example, the experience of envy. Envy is what I felt the other week when my friend turned up in her smart new sports car. I wanted one too, but it was a positive kind of envy. I was pleased that my friend was enjoying herself in her lovely car. I thought I would like a sports car but it would be impractical for me to have one, so I put the thought away. I am happy to get lifts with my friend whenever I can and have fun with her. Envy is a natural and normal emotion, and most people manage it in a positive way. In fact, envy can be a pow-erful motivator to get what you really want in life. However, we can-not all have what the other person has and being content with our lot in life is another form of self-regulation. (Have you noticed how many times we come back to regulation as the meaning of life?)

Children who have been severely deprived often react to envy in an aggressive or unhappy way and will react negatively to the smallest things they see. My perception is that when an abused and troubled child, sees another child looking happy, contented and relying on others, it is a particularly painful experience for them. We may won-der why the happy and contented child ends up getting whacked by the insecure and unhappy one. It is simply that secure children are immediately discernible by their sense of contentment, and it is that sense of contentment that a deprived child does not easily feel. So we need to show intense empathy for that child and the anger that arises when they meet secure children. Although we should not show approval if they hit another child, we should discuss their negative feelings, which may be represented in all sorts of ways. I often hear from carers whose children in their care have abused their pets. No doubt to many abused children it will be a shock to see that many animals are treated with more love and care than they have been. However, this is no excuse for causing harm and must be dealt with.

What we must do is notice this struggle and intervene for the child and help them understand these difficult feelings in a sensitive way. It is only with this intervention, help and support that the child is ever likely to make sense of their own dark feelings and emotions. Ultimately, these feelings will lead the child into disturbed and angry behaviour. This form of talking with a child about difficult things in their life is sometimes referred to as 'interactive repair'. It means that repair has to occur in interaction with somebody who cares enough to deal with it. As carers, we bother to interact. We talk about repair and we show the child what repair means. It does not matter if it does not work first time around. What really matters is that we are bothered. This is what alliance building is all about.

Small Clues that show the need to be connected to you

It is a powerful human biological need for children to be connected to an adult carer who protects them from all the difficulties of the world and provides for them adequately. When children appear not to display this innate need it is because something has gone very wrong in the adult's care of the child who feels they can no longer rely on adult care. It may well look as if the child does not want to form a connection with you, but it is a biological fact that they do – they simply have lost their sense that they need this connection. What you must do then is to respect that the child has lost this natural need (it's rather like losing your appetite when you are ill, which is another powerful natural force). They cannot have this foisted or imposed on them – it will appear very frightening and may seem like abuse again – i.e. being forced to do something about which they are frightened. We therefore have to take this one step at a time and this brings us back again to the concept of building an alliance rather than expecting a relationship. At the end of this session I will give you some ideas about alliance building.

It may be helpful to take note and explore the small cues that the child may give you that they do actually need you. It may be that you sit together and watch the same programme every day – a good, simple start to a sense of living together. The child builds in their mind that you enjoy sharing their world when it comes to, say, The Chuckle Brothers on television and they build in their mind the sense that you are there. You could make a point of not letting this time be disrupted – don't answer the phone and make it clear to others that this is an important part of the day. Equally, it could be that your child is more amenable at certain times of the day to small amounts of attention. They may like sitting in the kitchen and watching you cook. Notice too when your child is watching you. This particular attachment behaviour is sometimes uncomfortable for carers (they won't take their eyes off me'). In fact, this is reliable attachment behaviour and if you can possibly train yourself to tolerate it, you will make remarkable progress. The child is not being rude by staring – they are fascinated by you and by gazing at you they can start to take you into their life and heart. If possible, avoid making the child feel self-conscious about this activity.

Sensitivity counts in building a relationship

One of the clues from research about creating attachment relationships (especially in substitute care) is that 'care-giver sensitivity' will ultimately be the key factor in building a new relationship. This means that you are sensitive to the real needs of the child and the subtle cues that the child gives that say 'I really do need someone to care for me', even though everything else the child does rejects you. It is a big thing to ask a parent who is feeling rejected and bruised by a child's behaviour to be sensitive, especially if the child is not showing any sensitivity towards you. Ultimately, however, being sensitive to the child's needs is what counts. The exercises below may help you to rely on your own ability to be sensitively attuned to your child's needs at a time when everything else is saying 'run away'.

Below is a list of 'attachment clues' that you can look for that could give you hope on the days that are difficult and that might help you to look for something positive.

Alliance building is about one rule only – SAFETY

At the bottom of the alliance-building package that you want to build with your child on the basis that they cannot immediately build a relationship with you is a key word –'safety'. As we have already discussed, children who have disturbed behaviour don't feel safe most of the time and much of their time is spent defending themselves from an unsafe and unhappy inner world where many former abusers continue to lurk. We can guarantee that if your child is displaying bizarre behaviour, they feel unsafe about life – your care, people, school, sleep, etc. When you don't feel safe in life the whole nervous system is primed for fight or flight and you are in a state of nervous tension all the time, ready to defend yourself.

There can be all sorts of things in your child's life that signal that they feel unsafe, and you can hardly be blamed for not immediately knowing what these things are. For example, I worked recently with a child who hit his adoptive mother as she forgot to makes cakes to sell for charity at school. The boy had been in his placement for two years and was beginning to settle, so what had caused him to hit his mum? When we discussed the event, it emerged that this little boy had struggled to build his reputation at school as a 'good kid'. One of the things that had made him happy was that his adoptive mum had always produced great cakes for the sale and he had made the most money for charity. His whole being and status at school as far as he was concerned now rested on the quality of those cakes. He allowed himself to depend on her for his self-esteem at school. Fragile as it was, it was the start in building his self-esteem, but unfortunately his mum on this occasion had forgotten to make the cakes. His world dissolved into his former misery and he felt that he was no good at all. Worse still, he felt that his mother was unreliable. In his view she became the cause of his severe distress. In this instance his mum had to be a really big person. She had to make it clear that she would not tolerate being hit, but at the same time she had to make it clear that she completely understood that he felt let down and that this meant a lot to him. She understood the link in his mind that the cakes meant he belonged and if there were no cakes he did not belong so his world fell to pieces.

That is an example of how the smallest thing can trigger or stimulate your child's reactions. When their world is so fragile it can easily be shattered. It really could be down to the taste of a sweet that may stimulate traumatic recall (I discuss trauma in a later session) or the colour of a jumper you are wearing that may correspond with a previous carer's clothes. You will not know. The only thing you can do is to be continuously curious and creative about the way that you explore these episodes of upset with your child.

Beware of the Drama

As we discussed in an earlier session, some children gain attention through withdrawing their attachment signals. In fact, withdrawn children are actually trying to connect by minimising all their attachment signals as they think you will cope better. Equally, a child can choose to gain attachment relatedness through creating a huge drama with you. You will be the best assessor of this and no doubt you will be able to say straight away whether your child withdraws (because this is what they have learned is best) or whether they advance and make a huge muddled fuss with you in order to engage.

With the withdrawn child you have to struggle to look for those small clues about wanting to connect. The dramatic child will probably exhaust you and the tendency with such children is to want them to go away and get on with something else while you get your breath back. However, if a child is exhausting you, it is a very good signal that they are in need of a lot of the right attention rather than the wrong attention. The trouble is that such children (sometimes referred to in attachment theory as ambivalent) will get a lot of what they don't want instead of some of what they do want. Nobody wins. Often with the dramatic child it is best to try to decipher which of your behaviours helps the child feel secure and to give them a good piece of that every day in the right way, pointing out that this is because they are worthy of real attention – not the disorganised attention that they keep creating. Be careful too that you don't get caught in the drama of the dramatic child and become part of it. If you have that tendency – we all have tendencies – make a little study of your own behaviour and the way that you are stimulated into drama. Then make a plan for counteracting that.

TIME TO THINK

You may find your diary useful, but you may just want to make notes on some paper. The following questions are designed to help you to think and plan for building this alliance.

1   Can you list any of the obvious needs of your child when it comes to meeting their safety ideals? For example, do they need a night light? Do they appear insecure if you wander around in pyjamas? Conversely, do they ignore safety altogether and have no sense of danger – for example, no stranger danger, no traffic road sense, no sense of touching strange dogs? See if you can write down at least five ways in which you can help your child to feel safe or help them by demonstrating that their safety is your priority and that you are protecting them. The challenge is to demonstrate your concern for their safety at least once a day, but preferably more than this.

2   Do the child's requirements differ from your own values on safety? Try to see the difference. For example, you may think having a nice dark room is a great way to get to sleep. You may think that horse-riding is a brilliant experience and very safe. What are your own inner values on safety? Do you have a specific area of concern – for example, household fire? How do you deal with this? How do you demonstrate to the child in your care that you are viewing safety as a priority? Write yourself a few notes on how you can do this.

3   Write a mini dialogue in which you imagine you are having a conversation about safety with your child –about three sentences, but more if you want, in which you speak to them about your priority with regard to safety. See if you can use this dialogue on a regular basis. For example:

'Now make sure you switch off that plug when you've finished. We don't want you blowing yourself up, do we? We do everything in this house to make sure you are safe because we really care about you.'

Or

'No, you sit in the back of the car as we want to make sure you are safe while we are travelling. We don't want anything happening to you or we would be devastated.'

4   Can you name five ways in which you can lower your expectations of giving your child pleasure so that you don't overdose them with positive expectations? For example, could you stay home instead of go away on holiday and go for one-day outings instead of one great big outing for two weeks that might make your child feel insecure? This may seem hard on you, but I have met so many parents who have had a horrid long holiday with a child or children who are feeling insecure and would actually have preferred to have stayed home. Could you cook a nice meal at home instead of going out to a restaurant where a child can be bewildered by protocol, behave badly and make you feel awful? These bumper experiences could be your goal for the future when your child is settling down rather than something you must do now.

Rules for Building an Alliance and Demonstrating Safety to Your Child

The child in your care feels most vulnerable when they are encouraged to be in relationships with people. They don't feel vulnerable when they take care of themselves. Therefore, this has to be taken very slowly indeed. This may even be a signal for bizarre behaviour where the child is reminded that attachment is a signal for something dangerous. This will take months and years of help.

- You don't have to force the issue of attachment as this might be counterproductive and there is no research that upholds this strategy. You do have to offer the conditions for attachment – understanding and a knowledge of attachment relationships, constant understanding of the child's needs, making sense of behaviour, empathy, giving support, thinking about issues with the child, showing sensitivity to the child and attunement to their state of mind.

- You will have to repeat yourself daily. The child in your care will not learn from one conversation or comment. You will have to remind the child hundreds and hundreds of times that you are safe. You will have to be encouraging hundreds more times. Your child will gradually accept this and it will lay down new patterns of experience for them.

- The child in your care may shift position as in the 'Karpman Drama Triangle' described by Liotti (1999) from victim, to perpetrator, to rescuer. As your child shifts position, you will also be shifting position. You need to observe this and be clear about the role you might have been allocated. Do you really want to play the bad guy today?

- Don't make any attempt to resolve trauma until the alliance-building stage is completed. If the child has had traumatic experiences, this will come clear once the child is feeling safe and secure. They may then feel free to talk about bad experiences from the past. Don't force this issue. See the next session which describes trauma.

- It may help to remember that the child in your care may demonstrate their experience through 'acting out'. When children are acting out behaviour we know that they are not thinking about their behaviour. They act out as their thinking ability is impaired. We are aiming for reflection on behaviour. We may help our child by reflecting on their behaviour with them or even for them. One of my favoured ways to do this is by saying the following:

> *'I've been thinking about the way you hit your friend the other day. I wondered about that. I still can't quite work*

out what was going on. Have you had time to think more about that?'

Don't be afraid to show that you hold thoughts in your mind. One of the things that children do when they have not been cared for properly is to throw away thoughts very quickly. They may resist the fact that you choose to think about things, but don't let that stop you. Thinking and mindfulness are our goal here – you keep thinking. Badly treated children have not been shown that thinking really matters.

- Greet your child in a joyful way when you meet with them after a separation – i.e. when collecting them from school. In this way you are constantly re-enacting connectedness and showing that you want to be with them.

- Repair ruptures in the relationship as soon as realistically possible – i.e. after the child has done something wrong and received a consequence, gently discuss the reason for the rupture. You may have been cross about a particular incident, which is not a problem, but don't let it remain as a rupture for too long as this is what the child expects and their tendency to stay separate may feed on this exact expectation. As soon as you feel better (within a dignified amount of time for you), explain why you were cross and then move on.

- Reflect with the child as often as possible on their experience. Be conscious that the child in your care will resist this and may find it annoying or threatening. Show as much thoughtfulness as possible on both positive and negative behaviours.

- Make links between thinking and behaviour as often as possible. Keep this high on the agenda. For example, the child who hit his adoptive mother because she did not produce cakes as usual for the school sale. She made it clear that hitting was not acceptable but she also made it clear that she understood his fear that he would not be popular because he did not have cakes for the charity sale. Incidentally, he was not allowed to watch television for a week because he hit his mum, but she did repair the relationship.

Demonstrate that you take delight in considering safety issues in an age appropriate way. Keep this high on the agenda.

Even when it is difficult, affirm the child as much as possible. It is far easier for children in this state of mind to create neglect and hatred – this is their expectation of adults who care for them (i.e. it is their internal working model). You can expect to be tested. Take note and be mindful if the child has managed to overwhelm you with negative thoughts about themselves. It is just an old habit.

Don't forget to watch out for those odd little attachment clues (see the list below).

Avoid using terms of endearment until you are sure the child is feeling safe about your affection. Simply use the child's name until you are clear about this.

TIME TO THINK ABOUT CARE-GIVER SENSITIVITY

Part of building your alliance is to start to maximise opportunities to show sensitivity to your child's needs. You may find your diary useful for this exercise but you may just want to make notes on some paper. The following questions are designed to help you to think and plan for building care-giver sensitivity.

1 Are there any times when your child is calmer than others and more amenable to some positive input? Note down the exact times.

2 Are there any ways that you can show that you are available and thoughtful to your child at these times? For example:

   'Oh, look, we have a quiet moment. Is there anything I can help you with right now or would like to just enjoy some quietness?'

3   Is there anything that stops you being emotionally, physically and psychologically available at these times? Feel free to be honest with yourself – it's only you that has to read this. For example, you may feel grumpy because you have been rejected all day. You may feel thoroughly fed up and stressed. By now you may feel like rejecting the child yourself. At least get clear in your own mind what is getting in the way. I often explain to adoptive and foster parents that they are only human and are allowed their own moods but they should be aware that their own thoughts may be the barrier today.

4   Can you explain why the child might be more open to wanting to be connected at those times? Don't force an explanation but it might be obvious. For example, some children are more needy at bedtime and they try to stretch bedtime out so that they are not separated from you, indicating that they do need you. While you may well need to get time for yourself (as parents often do in the evenings), is there any way that you can put even a few more minutes of sensitive, kindly attention at that time of receptiveness on the part of the child? It could be just a few extra words of comfort.

5   Are there any aspects of the child's neediness at those times that are particularly annoying to you? Don't feel you are wrong if this is the case, but try to be aware of those dynamics again. For example, the child may sit and stare at you while you are working. You may find this too difficult. Is there anything you can offer as an alternative without rejecting the child's instinctive attachment behaviours?

That child may be thinking at those times how beautiful you are and how lucky they are to be in the house with you. That is such a special time. Don't forget that eye contact and smell are a very important aspect of attachment in infancy – note how babies use their eyes to track the behaviours of their parents for hours at a time and even the tiniest newborn can quickly identify the smell of their own mother. This is likely to be what your child is doing.

6   Use the timesheet and see if you can work with your partner/friend/supporter to plan in this specific time so that you can make use of it.

Here are some instinctive attachment behaviours that can be quite annoying, especially from older children who start to display them However, it could be such a positive start to attachment.

Attachment clues

Child is clingy.

Child is weepy.

Child constantly draws your attention to small insignificant things.

Child asks constant barrage of questions about small insignificant things.

Child asks for your help.

Child stares at you.

Child hangs around you.

Child smells you.

Child may lick you.

Child shows they have thought of you for a moment.

Child wants to be with you all the time and behaves like your shadow.

Child wants to know what you are talking about.

All of the above are understandably on the face of it odd behaviours, but they may be explainable by attachment neediness in the child. Obviously, you will only accept these behaviours to a level that is appropriate and comfortable.

Conclusion

In this session we have explored the idea of building an alliance with your child, with the notion of safety being the paramount feature of this alliance. We have thought about the idea that you may not be able to form an intense relationship with the child in your care for many reasons – the main one being that the child is afraid of intensely close relationships because of past negative experiences. So the child's own sense of safety is the priority rather than a close relationship. We looked at the possibility that your idea of safety may be very different from that of a child who is very damaged and traumatised. Once you have an alliance in place or a 'secure base' you may be able to go onto the next stage of looking for the subtle cues that the child sends out at certain times in order to get close to you.

SESSION SEVEN

ACTING OUT AND MANAGING EMOTIONS

MANAGING RELENTLESS BEHAVIOUR IS THE PATHWAY TO SUCCESS

IDENTIFYING UNDERLYING STATES OF MIND

In my work as an Adoption Support Agency in the United Kingdom, the most frequent problem that adoptive parents and foster parents have to consider is the 'relentless' fashion of their child's behaviour. By this I mean that the behaviour occurs again and again or that emotional states arise repeatedly for hours at a time. This is often exhausting for parents who have to tolerate extreme states of mind when they cannot even understand them. It may feel like being held hostage by the child.

Some parents have told me that it is very helpful when I can witness those states of mind with the parent so that I can reassure them that it is not themselves who are going mad. Some parents feel that this sort of behaviour isolates them from friends with children who do not have unmanageable, highly charged emotions. They might have to make a sudden hasty exit with a screaming child who may continue to scream for an hour. I would just like to say to all parents who are reading this that whenever I have shared this experience with parents, I do know how hard it can be. A little girl came to my office recently and gave a hearty demonstration of the disregulated states that her mother had been telling me about for weeks. It was as if she really wanted me to know about it. I was delighted to share the experience with her mum in order to support her, but I must say that I did have a headache for the rest of the day! This adoptive mother was coping with such behaviour nearly every day.

Similarly, the adoptive mother who helped me with my research went through the same experience. Her little adoptive son demonstrated an extreme and relentless state to three adults for an hour and a half when none of us could do anything to calm him. All of us were experts in child behaviour! We were exhausted and it took us days to work out this state of mind. Essentially, it looked as if he would not give in to adults, but it is more likely that he could not give in as he was too afraid. Perhaps this session might give you a sense that you have a witness to those times that are so very bewildering and that might leave you isolated and feeling useless, helpless and exhausted. I truly believe how hard this is for you. It is a common feature of badly abused children and you are not alone.

From my research in *How Do We Help Children with Extreme Behavioural Difficulty?* (North, 2009), I discovered that the issue with these states of distress is that they are the eye of the storm, they are the snapshot of the child's inner world, whereas we might like to think that it will stop or go away. The fact is that those chronically disturbed and distressing states will never go away until we have deeply understood them and met the child where they are trapped in distress, fear and turmoil. This is all that they are showing us. It is they who are held hostage with these inner states and they are trying to let us know about this.

They are also showing that they don't have the capacity to regulate those states. They don't have a thermostat to say 'that is done now'. If you took a perfectly healthy child and ignored their needs chronically over a short period of time and left them feeling isolated and alone, they too would emerge with this behaviour. It is a horrible thought, I know, but the fact is that children who act out in this way are suspended in time and space with the sense that there is never anyone coming to meet their needs. They are also defended from receiving help when it actually comes that they cannot see, hear or feel the soothing that you are trying to offer. Not surprisingly, parents feel defeated and just want to put an end to the noise. Children who fall into these states do not have any mechanism inside that self-regulates. The state also may not be about noise, crying or anger – it may simply be a state of extreme resistance to adult presence or care.

Again, if you take a perfectly normal, securely attached seven-year-old who gets upset about something, they may cry for a while. If they are secure they will seek out their main attachment figure instinctively when they are upset. Their parent will help to solve their problem or soothe their emotions through parental empathy, understanding and mindfulness, and within an hour or so an episode of upset will be over and a plan made for the parent to understand and solve the child's problem. This occurs often in childhood. A child may be upset for a short while many times a week. The parent who is mindful is there to support and say 'It's OK. I'm here to help and I love to help you.' Over time the seven-year-old gets better and better at internalising this experience and by the time he is a teenager he may well feel he wants to be more independent and not go to his mum or dad for support but proudly regulates his own emotions or goes to his mates for help. Such a teenager will have acquired the confident notion that upset states can be soothed and he will enter adulthood and hopefully have the autonomy to repeat the same sense of soothing with his own children.

This is the main finding that emerged from my research and it was the main feature of John Bowlby's research into childhood attachment, which was to listen to the child's emotions. It is where childhood exists. All our knowledge about self-regulation is in our memory from our infancy with our parents. Our caring parents helped us to calm and soothe our upset and distress. If we had dismissing parents or unreliable parents, perhaps we found soothing from another figure. The fact is that a baby simply cannot soothe their own emotions. A baby cannot survive without the attention of an adult. They always need someone there to engage in the task with them. The parent and child are engaged in an intense relationship where every minute of the infant's life says 'Make sure you are there to care for me.' And, of course, babies can only communicate through crying or displaying that they are content. There is little territory in between. A six-month-old does not say 'OK mum, I'll hold back on the screaming until you feel able to get here.' A six-month-old baby will scream their head off and that screaming says 'Get here now or I will die.'

When we care for a troubled child there is every chance that their emotions and inner life and experience will have been entirely neglected. I have never met a child yet who came into care because their inner life was intact. This means that your child's brain has developed with the expectation that no one will come to help them. They will probably only stop crying when they are so exhausted that they cannot cry any longer – this is the usual pattern of behaviour. It takes minutes to frighten the life out of an infant by leaving them for too long without attention. The infant feels abandoned and cannot self- soothe. So, in short, those emotions are there for a reason – to stay alive. When your child is in one of those unsoothable emotional states, that too is about staying alive, but in a very distorted way. When your child is caught in that state they truly believe that no one will come to help them. At those times it is probably hard for them to believe that anyone will come along and help you with the problem.

So how do we take control of this significant problem? The first thing we have to do is to start to see these opportunities for what they are – the child in need of help. It is not a child wanting to be naughty and make you feel bad. The child is caught in the stressful margin between care and not care. The first start, then, is to adjust your capacity to think about this and provide a secure base so that you can say to the child that you are always there for them and that you are willing to try very hard to understand their emotions. Whatever the emotional climate of the child – wailing, distress, despair, rage – your state of mind remains the same: 'I understand that you want to communicate with me and I am right here for you.' However, you are allowed to leave the room for five minutes to catch your breath or make a cup of tea if it helps you with this stance or just helps you to calm yourself. You could even call a friend for support or take some time for a few deep breaths.

Track the child's Moods

The second thing that you can do is start to track these emotional states, which can be very helpful to you over time. However, you should track all the child's states of mind throughout the day, not just their emotional states. You can create a sort of daily temperature chart for the child or children in your care of their emotional states. I have provided a chart for you in this session. You need a page for each day of the week and I suggest that you track your child's moods and emotions for a month and then take some time to look at typical outbursts and see if there is a pattern to them. Another way to do this if you are more of a 'words person' is to keep a daily diary of the child's moods, which is just as effective. Alternatively, you could do both. The chart was originally the idea of Ros and Jeremy Holmes who wrote the *The Good Mood Guide. How to turn your bad moods into good moods* (Holmes, 1993). I can thoroughly recommend this

	8	12	4	8	Observations and comments in relation to daily chart
Date:					
Time	8	12	4	8	
Mood					
Happy					
Relaxed/calm					
Playful					
Affectionate					
Hurt					
Compliant					
Envious					
Coercive					
Manipulative					
Despairing					
Despondent					
Abusive/rude					
Aggressive					
Angry / rage					
Out of control					
Anxious					
Frustrated					
Argumentative					
Subdued / quiet					
Depressed					
Exitable / hyper					
Shameful					
Sad					
Frightened					
Self harm					
Suicidal					
Grief					

Mood Chart

book if you want to read more about mood management. I developed the idea as I thought it would be helpful for parents to have guidelines for the range of extreme emotions that children can feel at these times.

The chart will give you some sense of managing these states from more of a distance and give you a sense of better management of them. You also need to be able to record as accurately as possible the length that a state lasts for. There is a big difference when a state of mind reduces from one hour to, say, forty minutes, especially if you are on the other end of the experience. You then have a basis from which you can begin to give some feedback to your child and hold a conversation about their emotional state. I always say to people that it is far easier to talk about these things when you are not actually in the eye of the storm. It is impossible when a child is completely lost to you in a despairing state of emotion to ask 'I wonder what this is about?' And here is my opportunity to advise you never do that. Just put in the soothing. The time to discuss 'what this is all about' is later when the child is feeling better.

As is usual with all aspects of your child's behaviour, check out exactly how you are feeling about their state of mind. Does it frighten you, make you feel depressed, angry, panic stricken, etc.? Get clear how you feel and settle that feeling as soon as you can. You cannot really deal with this if you are disturbed yourself. Keep a mood chart for yourself and track your responses to the child. This would be a brilliant way to keep yourself alert to what is happening emotionally in your household. Better still, everyone in the house could be responsible for their own mood chart, especially with older children. It could be something to share at the end of the day.

The Five Rs and Interactive Repair

When a child is in an emotional state aim to stay with them – don't move away from them or abandon them. Try to give them the right amount of the right attention and don't ignore them or walk out on them. Most of all, to try to keep your head when the child is definitely losing theirs. I find it helps to think of this task as the five Rs – i.e. receive, regulate, repair, resolve and repeat. You also need to do this within a framework of 'interactive repair' in that you need to be with the child and connected to them to help their emotional states and to make them realise that people really do want to help. It is the ultimate belief of such children that people don't really want to help them and they are not worthy of help. You have to interrupt that idea and the strategy is as follows:

The Five Rs

> *Help the child to know that you have **R**eceived the emotion they are communicating.*

> *Help the child with **R**egulation of the state by soothing.*

> *Help **R**epair their connection with you by more soothing and understanding.*

> *Help provide **R**esolution to that continuous state of despair.*

> *Expect to **R**epeat the experience again and again.*

The relentlessness of these emotions is partly due to the fact that no one will actually 'receive' the message in the child's emotions. Children communicate when people receive their emotions. Adults, especially loving and concerned parents, feel these communications from children. They think about the state and then they provide the resolution. They have received that emotion and taken it into them-selves. Often with these children their emotional state is so bad that no one could possibly want to receive the emotion – it is too much to handle. However, it is the only real way to do this. Resolution is the long-term goal. It may take years, but what you are looking for is a resolved state of mind. You can expect to repeat the experience many times. Imagine how many times a day the mother of a well-cared for baby will run to her offspring to help repair and resolve their little problem. Then imagine how much of this the child in your care did not get and be proud that you are giving them this attention now.

TIME TO THINK ABOUT THE FIVE Rs

First of all, let's think about you. How do you work emotionally? How much attention do you need emotionally? Think of a time when you were very upset in your life. An incident that may have distressed you. Perhaps something that felt it was unjust or unfair. Don't spend too long dwelling on the detail of this – we don't want to make you miserable here. What is more important is to remember how you resolved this emotional upset.

Did someone come along and talk to you in a kind way?

Did you seek help from someone?

Were you upset for a long time?

The point of prompting your memory here is to help you to resonate with the experience of what soothed you. Do you still get upset by that incident? For example, if it was a matter of grief and loss of a loved one, you could easily still feel upset months and even years later. There is no problem with this, but it is an excellent opportunity to note how it takes time and patience to resolve these issues.

Now let's work on the Rs. Here are some notes that may help you.

The Five Rs of Interactive Repair

Receive – what you need to remember

Here we mean that the child tries to get someone (undoubtedly you as their primary carer) to receive and understand their emotional and mental state. We all need to do this and children do it all the time. This means that you are sensitive to the child's feeling or mental state inside yourself and you reflect on it; then you act for the child to support that experience. Sometimes that state with a child who has been abused is so traumatic and difficult that we actually don't want to receive it because it is too much for us. We want to protect ourselves from it. This is entirely under-standable. Let's think about what you can accept and receive by answering some questions.

- ⊃ What do you think your child is trying to communicate in these states?

- ⊃ Do you have a story attached to those emotions that gives it some meaning for you?

- ⊃ How do you think your child feels at those times? What are your thoughts?

- ⊃ Try to think about how much you need to defend your-self from those difficulties. Understandably, if the child is aggressive or about to harm you, you will have to make yourself and the child safe. After you have done that, what are you left understanding?

- ⊃ Once the child is settled, can you talk to them about that state of mind?

What are your automatic thoughts around the child's states and emotional experiences? See if you can capture at least five. Here are some possibilities:

- ⊃ *Oh no, here we go again – not another one.*

- ⊃ *What is that child on about now? We only dealt with this the other day.*

- ⊃ *I can't stand this any more. I really cannot take any more.*

- ⊃ *How much longer am I going to have to put up with this?*

There is absolutely nothing wrong with these thoughts – they are entirely natural. However, if you countered those thoughts with thoughts that were understanding, accepting and receiving, you might have to work at it. Even if it is through gritted teeth, those thoughts could shift the experience a little:

⊃ *You poor child – this upsets you so much.*

⊃ *It looks like it's that thought or that memory that's upsetting you again.*

⊃ *I know this will take a long time to resolve. There's no one else who can do it but me.*

⊃ *We will have to face up to this for as long as it takes.*

Sometimes I tell adoptive parents, foster parents and carers 'Fake it till you make it.' That is a saying from Alcoholics Anonymous where they encourage participants to pretend they can do the task, even if they feel they cannot. In doing this it convinces the mind to accept the task. It really is OK to fake it until you really get it. It may take a few weeks to convince yourself that you really believe that attention and receptiveness will be the resolution. Name five of your automatic thoughts and then counter these with receptive terminology.

Finally, I am aware that you may need a break if your child is in a relentless emotional state, otherwise you may become distressed yourself or get a headache. I am also aware that it could go on for hours. You must factor in your own needs here. I think it is perfectly feasible to take a break if you need to, but always do this in a way that does not leave the child feeling abandoned. So tell them where you are going, how long you will be and why you are doing it.

Regulate

This is where we offer the child our help in regulating their emotions. It does not matter if it fails to work and we don't get a regulated child immediately but it is our ultimate goal.

Crying Child For the upset child, this is slightly easier. We say soothing things and hold their hand if that is safe for them. What I would say about the crying child is to allow a certain amount of sympathy and empathy so that they relieve their feelings. If it comes to a point – say, after about a couple of hours or so where the child is not regulating, then I suggest you say to the child,

'I'm going to help you to stop now because it is not good for you to cry for so very long.' Try to do things like sit the child up, fetch a warm drink and slightly distract them from the focus of upset. In my experience, to allow the crying to continue for hours and hours with buckets of your empathy will do two things. It will exhaust you and it will not help the child to regulate or get the idea that emotions can be regulated.

In order to prepare yourself for your next episode, write a mini speech that you can repeat to your child. This means a few sentences that are soothing, kind and show that you are there to help. For example:

'I am right here for you and I know just how you feel right now. You are so upset and you feel that no one cares but I do and I care very much. We will work this out together.'

Once you have done this, write a mini speech a couple of sentences long that show how to move the child on from their tearful and upset state. For example:

'You've been crying for an hour and I'm going to help you move on from those upset thoughts now because you need a little rest from them. We can think about those things another time and I have got them in my mind now so I can think about them too and help you. I'm going to get your favourite drink. How brilliant that you have been able to let me know just how upset you feel inside. I really feel I can help you now.'

Child in a rage The best response is not the most obvious because rage can be very frightening, especially if you have a child who is turning over their room ('trashing' is the popular term) or breaking your windows or kicking the back of your car seat while you are driving (stop the car under these circumstances). It is especially frightening if you have not experienced a lot of rage from people or indeed if you have been the subject of abusive rage in your life. It might help you to explore that and overcome it, but not while the child's rage is going on.

Try to write down a mini conversation for soothing a child in a rage. For example:

'I know you are angry about something. How very difficult for you. I really want to try to understand what that is. Can you tell me more about it as I think I can help you? When you feel ready, we will talk about it. Do you need some space or shall I stick with you for a while?'

Resistant/domineering state   The key with resistance is not to engage with it and always to lower your own threshold. A child who becomes intractable and intransigent is very probably frozen to the spot and terrified. Always think 'lower the barrier'. Have a calm, sympathetic voice and face but don't become part of the child's resistance. The child may issue unreasonable demands such as 'go away, go away' and of course this is difficult with a small child as you will be watching for safety. However, you can respond by saying, for example, 'Alright, darling, I will move to one side until you feel better. I can't go totally away as I have to make sure you're safe.'

See if you can write your own narrative for this type of situation. For example:

'You poor old thing – that must be such a difficult set of feelings for you. I will just go and get the washing in and pop back and see how you are doing. Just as soon as you are feeling better we can do something nice together. I think you can't tell me about it now as you are feeling so cross, but never you mind. I think you and I can get there.'

Repair and Resolve

To some extent, just being there for the child is the key. Repair and resolve usually come after the emotional crisis and it could be that you cannot repair and resolve things straight away. However, if your child's outburst has been because of a broken computer game or something that the child perceives to be unfair, then let it be so. If you put in a sanction of no television because your child has been very unkind to your pet and as a result you have to deal with two hours of relentless behaviour, then that also has to be so. The resolve and repair here lie in not giving in on your decision but in your explanation about your decision. For example:

> *'I know that is hard for you, but I can't let you think it's OK to break things like that. I know you don't like it when I say no. It's one of the things I am helping you with.'*

The issue of your child's regulation of that state is a separate matter from the here and now issue of what triggered it and is part of an ongoing larger conversation with your child when they are feeling better and more receptive to thinking about how they want to have help with managing those times. When your child is not deeply distressed and upset could be a good time to talk about what helps them the most and what sort of thoughts they might be thinking that lead them to such unresolvable despair. Either way, the skill is in giving the child a sense that you are joining up the experience and making sense of it with them. You are showing them that at those dreadful times that they are worthy of adult care and understanding.

Repeat

You cannot repair the internal world of your child by one endeavour. As we have said, it is a process not an event. You will need to be able to repeat this cycle of behaviour many times in order to help your child to internalise a new experience that works in their favour. If you can adjust your mindset to the relentlessness of this task, you may even start to feel that you are in command of the process, rather than that your life is being taken over by a monstrous intrusion. If you can manage this aspect of your child's inner life, you can at least be satisfied that you are attending to the most important aspect of their life and helping to make a big change.

Conclusion

In this session we have discussed the idea of performing the seemingly impossible task of understanding the depths of despair in your child and how this despair gets acted out in relentless behaviour. Hopefully, you may have discovered that it is not at all impossible to understand that despair. If we frame the picture on relentless behaviour, it is the key to everything else that we do. It is the long-term task of caring for a child with difficult behaviour.

SESSION EIGHT

UNDERSTANDING TRAUMA and SHAME

Once the alliance is built, the processing of traumatic experiences may begin

We have talked about building an alliance with a child in contrast to entering into an intensely affectionate relationship too quickly, especially if children have been harmed by adults and suffered from neglect. We have considered the idea that such children find it hard to consider adults to be a source of continuous and reliable support, as any secure child might naturally expect. Forming an alliance in which safety for the child is presented as the priority is a way to begin to prove to the child that adults can be reliable.

Once children have established a deeper sense that the world is a safer place with some safe people and is beginning to enjoy life, it is possible that they may begin to 'process' some of their bad experiences. Unfortunately, this does not happen to order, so I cannot give you a plan for this occurrence. It could happen within weeks of the child arriving in your home because they quickly understand that you are reliable. It could also take months or years. There is no right or wrong about how a child makes the decision that it is safe to rely on adults again and you will recall that this is never a single decision – it is a matter of small decisions over time. Moreover, when children start to feel able to love an adult again and show affection their emotions come to life and it is possible that they can 'deal with' many more previously blocked emotional issues. When I use the word 'process' here I am referring to the idea that experiences that have been locked away start to come to the surface of the mind so that they can be reconsidered or managed with the new parent. Our brains are built to process experience and put that experience in place in an organised way. We have the ability to think about our experience and make sense of our lives. This is called 'reflective functioning' (Fonagy, 1997).

It would seem that with children who have had no opportunity for help, they cease to think about life, behaviour and experience, and therefore simply react to everything that comes their way. This is the cause of a lot of difficult behaviour in troubled children. They simply have not been taught or shown that it is possible to think about things and change them. Another cause of reactive and impulsive behaviour in children is trauma. There is a great deal of talk about trauma and I think that many parents are afraid of the idea that their child may have been traumatised. We never talk about trauma in an ordinary way – we only hear about it when some poor person has overreacted due to post-traumatic stress and possibly caused severe harm.

Our brains are built to function and cope with difficult experiences, and the brain functions particularly well at doing this when children are secure. There is all the back-up of secure and safe experience locked into the thinking of a secure child, and they can fall back on many good and supportive memories when things go wrong. That is not to say, of course, that secure children will never experience any trauma, because no one has control over accidents or events that may shock us. It is just to say that notable research shows that a more secure inner thermostat is likely to cope better with trauma (Van der Kolk, 1996).

Again, we are built to cope with difficult situations and we are programmed to defend ourselves in the event of anything that is life-threatening. There is a part of the brain called the amygdala (pronounced 'amigdala') that is designed to sound the alarm in the event of danger. When primitive man saw a dinosaur coming over the horizon, the amygdala alarm would sound and he had two responses. He would either fight the dinosaur or he would run away from it. His reactions no doubt served him very well as primitive man evolved into the sophisticated human being of modern times . Our brains remain much the same, however, except that the thinking process that enables us to think and plan ahead (known as the prefrontal cortex) has grown in size, as has our capacity to think.

The alarm system in the brain remains much the same as it was for primitive man. It goes off like a highly tuned smoke sensor at the notion of danger and our internal system gets ready to fight or run away (fight or flight). So we become alarmed in situations that we perceive to be dangerous, and the heart starts pumping ready for the fight or flight response. Then our thinking mind will click into place and check the environment and says 'No, it's OK, it's safe – you're OK' and the body calms down again. All is well and the amygdala will serve us well as long as our thinking system can work effectively by resetting the thermostat to 'calm' for us when all is safe. People who can keep their head in a difficult situation effectively can perform remarkable feats even though the alarm system is rightly setting off the fight or flight response.

A remarkable example of this type of experience took place in January 2009 when Flight 1549 piloted by Flight Captain P. Sullenberger was taking off from La Guardia Airport in America to fly to Charlotte Airport with 155 passengers on board. All of the plane's engines failed shortly after take-off. Realising that he had no choice but to make a crash landing, Captain Sullenberger pinpointed in his mind the Hudson River as the safest place to land in order to avoid civilian fatalities as well as save the lives of his passengers. He made a text-book landing on the River Hudson and everyone on board was collected within minutes by waiting boats who had been warned of the landing by air-traffic control. As it happened, Captain Sullenberger was trained to keep his head in an emergency and it was his quick thinking and control of the situation that saved many lives. The passengers on his aircraft were landed safely, evacuated the craft and put to shore. Most of them did not even get their feet wet as a result of the incident! Here is an example of how the prefrontal cortex (i.e. our thinking) can take charge when we have been trained or shown how to think straight. Captain Sullenberger later said that he felt sick to the pit of his stomach and was terrified. However, he overrode this fear and got on with the job of saving his passengers. This could be called a miracle, but it was a very good example of mind over amygdala. It shows that the children in our care can gradually learn to control their hyper-alert alarm systems if they are trained properly. We as carers can model this process. Just keep Captain Sullenberger to the front of your mind!

The problem with trauma arises when the amygdala stays alarmed and alert and is unable to receive a message from the thinking brain that there is no longer any danger. That is traumatic stress. The alarm system just won't calm down and danger is perceived when actually it is not there. That, of course, is the problem with the children in our care. They are alarmed when danger is not there and their minds have not been taught to recover from that stress. Hence for them everyday life is like a plane crash with no Sullenberger in the pilot's seat.

How Trauma Can Affect Young Minds forever

Understanding how unresolved trauma contributes to complex and overwhelming behaviour in children could be important in helping us to know how to recognise dissociative states such as trances and freezing. This is when children appear not to be coping with reality and their mind seems to be somewhere else. Such is the case with the young people we care for who have been exposed to overwhelming experiences with no chance of anyone helping them to calm down. Traumatic or overwhelming events cause a shock to the nervous system. It is natural for the mind and body to process everyday events but sometimes an event may occur that overwhelms the coping or processing capacity of the brain and nervous system, and cannot be psychologically processed and completed. This is referred to as trauma.

For a child, a traumatic event may constitute anything obvious from being physically or sexually abused by an adult, but we tend to forget that angry parents can be very frightening to a child. So, a parent who cannot regulate their anger can frighten and shock a child on a regular basis. Parents therefore provide an environment that actually causes trauma rather than normal development. The child cannot make sense of this and it becomes trapped in their mind. Thus, trauma causes an imbalance in the nervous system and may cause a child to display some of the following behaviours:

- hyperalertness
- overcaution
- excessive fear
- overreaction

- excessive anxiety

- excessive anger

- wanting to frighten others

- cruel behaviour

- bizarre behaviour

- continuous (not just occasional) bad dreams

- extreme fear of going to bed alone

- inability to to play easily

- not appearing to live in reality

- obvious dissociative states (i.e. not appearing to be in reality)

A traumatic event stays in the mind and blocks everyday thinking. This is why a child's thinking processes can become distorted when they have experienced trauma. They cannot think clearly and often this is reflected in their behaviour which may be strange or bizarre. A trauma also often creates a train of negative thought towards the self. Events that occur that are similar to the traumatising event then restimulate the memory of the original event that is caught in the mind. Even if the triggering event is very mild, it may stimulate a reaction that is as strong as the original trauma. So if a child is abused by a man in a bright red jumper, it is possible that bright red jumpers might signal danger to that child in the future. Trauma can be restimulated by thoughts, images, emotions or sensations. As a carer, you may wear your favourite bright red jumper and wonder why the child you are caring for is suddenly in a rage – their trauma has been restimulated.

The adult caring for the child may then find them acting in a strange or disproportionate way to a minor event that has restimulated the trauma. The soothing function of the central nervous system cannot extend itself to the traumatic experience that is stored in the traumatic memory. Some traumas can resolve over time as the child becomes older. They may reflect on the experience and find that they can think about it in a soothing and calm way or put it in its place in their mind. Thus, they have 'processed' the trauma. For example, a child of five who was physically abused by excessive slapping may blame themselves. However, at the age of 16, they may be able to put it into perspective and realise that it was because they were living with a stressed and depressed parent. It may start to make more sense to them and the brain will start to make connections again. This young person may be able to tell themselves that all is safe in their world now (especially if they have had good care) and they will cease to be hyperalert.

There is no reason why a child should wait until they are older to process trauma. There are many ways that adults can help to support a child who has been traumatised. A starting point is to think of this as something that can be managed rather than something strange and out of the ordinary. There are many methods to help children overcome trauma – for example, Bessel van der Kolk, who is one of the world's leading researchers into trauma, has recently observed that yoga and drama therapy can be very useful to help children and adults to calm their central nervous system and allow the trauma to release from the mind in a gradual way.

Ultimately, trauma affects a child's functioning, emotion regulation and psychological development, including physical development. The overall impact of trauma is that the child does not develop to their full potential.

Supporting a Child with Trauma

1   Ask for professional help from a psychologist, psycho-therapist or psychiatrist who is experienced in treating children with trauma as soon as you start to observe trau-matised behaviours like those listed above. The gateway is through your GP or the child's social worker. Seek specific psychological treatment. Treatment such as eye move-ment desensitisation and reprocessing (otherwise known as EMDR) are highly effective with children. See if you can keep a diary of times that the child displays this behaviour as it could help to contribute to a speedier diagnosis.

2   Once you have done this, remember that you can be help-ful by being very soothing to the child and talking about their behaviours and helping them to be aware of what

they are doing. Do this when you feel calm and do it in a non- judgemental, thoughtful and enquiring way. For example:

> *'I notice you get really angry every time I am a little bit late [the child may fear being abandoned again]. I am so sorry to upset you by being late. I am not going to leave you alone for ever – I promise – poor old you, thinking I was going to leave you there. Next time I will try to be on time. Just try to remember that I am here for you and this house is safe now but you may have memories from the past about people leaving you on your own and that might make it worse.'*

3   If your child wants to talk with you about their experience, let them do this. For example, one adoptive parent I work with served her child a wonderful English breakfast one morning. The child could have been overjoyed but he started to cry as he remembered a time that his birth mother sat and ate breakfast and gave him nothing. The foster parent sat him on her lap and cuddled him and explained that this would never happen in her house and she reminded him of thee three sausages, double egg and double hash browns that were on the table before him. Eventually, he ate them and enjoyed them, but what was more important was the intimate opportunity in which the new adoptive parent could soothe her child's distress and pain by interacting with him rather than dismissing his distress. These mini opportunities are the building-blocks of resolution and repair for the child.

4   As the quality of your relationship increases and as the child feels safer, so their traumatic memories are more likely to emerge – this is simply because the brain has a self-healing mechanism that recognises immediately when there is an opportunity for safety and resolution. It seems there is a tendency for us to want to heal. Some new adoptive and foster parents are dismayed because bizarre behaviour starts to emerge just as they thought the child was feeling happy. The rule is that you can expect traumatic memories to arise for the child.

5   As traumatic memories arise, simply be willing to receive them for the child (remember the 5 Rs) and don't be afraid of the traumatic memory yourself – it is the child who is afraid of the traumatic memory. The rules are thus:

Listen

Accept

Repeat back to the child all that you heard

Tell the child that you are glad you have been told and now you can share it with them, and that they will start to feel better now that they have shared their painful thoughts: 'You are so clever to have told me so that I can help you.'

Don't dwell on the subject for any longer than the child needs but give it enough time to show that you are there with them. Let the child put those exposed memories away again as soon as they want. Give the child soft positive attention and always remind them that they are safe now. That is the key.

End the episode of 'telling' with positive emotional reinforcement such as a hug or hand-holding, or a positive comment or positive thought if your child does not accept physical contact from you.

6   Do continue with psychological support – together foster parents, adoptive parents and carers in general can help children to live through their trauma and live a care-free life.

7   Don't attempt to grasp at bringing the child's trauma to the surface yourself. This will lead to fear and mental pain. They will talk to you when they are safe and only if they want to. You can only really provide a safe, warm and sensitive environment that gives the child a sense of safety and co-operation. When children feel safe they will be safe to talk about their fears.

8   Do watch for any trauma in our own system. You may have suffered mild trauma or even extreme trauma. You can be restimulated by your child's trauma find yourself getting

upset when your child gets upset. Don't be afraid to get this treated if it is severe. Again, there are treatments that should help you and some counselling sessions from your GP can be just as effective as some of the more modern treatments such as EMDR.

TIME TO THINK ABOUT TRAUMA

You will be accustomed now to the idea that this section is designed to help you reflect on yourself and your own thinking in relation to the child in your care. Your diary may be useful for notes that you write. These questions are designed to prompt your thinking about trauma. Obviously, this is for your own personal use and if you feel that you are trying to cope with too much at present to think about such things and that this will make you feel bad or upset or stimulate too much emotion, then you will be very sensible and in charge of yourself to put the exercise to one side. Simply read the above material on trauma so that you are well informed and possibly leave this exercise until you feel as if you can handle it. One of the keys to good self-regulation (and calm emotions) is to know your limitations so, if you are going to put this exercise to one side, consider yourself to be practising your self-regulation instead and well done you for recognising what you can and cannot do!

How have you dealt with trauma?

1   Can you name the three most extreme or traumatic or deeply upsetting experiences in your own life?

2   How did you recover from these experiences? Take one experience and write down the details of getting to feel better:

   How did it affect you?

   How long did it take?

Who helped you?

On reflection, how do you feel about this incident now?

Do you think this is a resolved trauma?

If you feel you have any seriously unresolved trauma that deeply affects you and that your child may restimulate in you, you have a choice about how you deal with it. I would advise that it is a fairly straightforward matter to deal with such matters. Your GP may be able to refer you to a surgery therapist or you may be able to find a private therapist. I would also advise that I meet a lot of adoptive and foster parents who have old traumas restimulated by the extreme traumas with which their children are living and once we discover this is happening, we can actually put it back in its box quite quickly and parents are surprised at what a difference this can make to their own thinking.

To complete this exercise, take a few moments to focus your mind on the happiest event in your life. Think about the people there and how you felt. Let yourself feel some positive emotions for a while before you move on. This will move your mind on from having focused on distress. This is another example of mind management.

About your child

1   How frequently do you see your child overreacting in a way that might be restimulated trauma – i.e. unreasonable responses?

2   Do you feel that this is a matter of soothing, support and conversation from you, or do you feel that it needs more serious clinical attention? If it is the latter, I would suggest that you contact the child's adoption/fostering social worker and ask if they can make a referral for clinical help. This assumes that in discussion, the child in your care would actually like this or, you

may make this decision for them because they are too young to make it for themselves.

3   Can you describe in a few sentences what it is that you think your child is acting out? Do you have evidence of past experiences that you believe to be traumatic to the child?

4   To what extent have you been able to externalise and think about this with your child? Obviously this depends on their age.

5   To what extent are you satisfied that you are able to support and apply the five Rs – i.e. receive, regulate, repair, resolve, repeat - to this situation? If you are satisfied that you can contain this experience without it causing distress to you or other members of your family, that may be enough. If you feel you need more help, then you probably do need more help. This can be located within the community or through a Post Adoption Support Agency. These can be found on the internet and the local authority that has placed the child should be the source of funding for this help. With some tenacity, admittedly, help is available. However, this is a clinical condition and social workers and doctors should be your first port of call for assistance.

Shame and Consequences – another cause of difficult behaviour

Some foster parents, adoptive parents and carers get very frustrated as the children in their care appear to have no sense of shame regarding their behaviour. Here is an explanation for this which has been provided by the neurobiologist Allan Schore (Schore, 2003)

Shame is an emotional state that emerges in infants as part of their neurological and emotional development. It is a significant milestone in infant development. It is also a development that requires very sensitive management so that the infant can 'autoregulate' their shame system. In other words, it is crucial that a sensitive carer joins with the child in learning how to accept shame as part of a self-regulating system. (Schore 2003)

Shame is effectively a warning signal that helps us to know when we are about to do something which others will not approve of. If you think for a moment about the last time you felt shame, it's uncomfortable even to think about. However, there is no doubt that the flash of biological heat – the redness of the face, the sharpness of breath, butterflies in the stomach – will have an impact and you will say to yourself 'I don't like experiencing that'.

Infants develop shame with a sense of connection to their primary carer – assuming that all is well in the relationship and there is a secure attachment. There is a sense of attunement or even a grace and musicality to the interactions between the parent and child. When this attunement is suddenly pierced by the parents' disapproval the infant will be very surprised indeed and experience a sudden shock that their world can be dissolved by the parent's disconnection from them or displeasure. The toddler does not like it and is probably upset.

A well-attuned parent will help the child to cope with this moment of fracture to their relationship. They will gently repair that fracture with soothing words and explanations. For example: 'Well, you really can't put that truck in the electric socket – that's why mummy shouted.' The child is reverted to their connected world and all is well. However, the surprise of mother's disapproval, the usual state of happiness broken and the discomfort – all help the infant to remember that the truck and the electric socket are not a good idea and that people in the outside world will disapprove.

Measured amounts of shame are helpful to the infant's socialisation and development of conscience. Interestingly, the infant usually starts to experience shame once they are independent in their actions and it often emerges when the infant learns to walk and becomes a toddler. Toddlers are notably rather thrilled by the prospect of exploring their environment and it is at this time that mum or dad has to put a stop to certain activities. The infant then starts to learn to accept restriction.

The problem arises when parents are insensitive. They may yell too loudly, they may smack too hard, they may not repair the rupture that occurs in the relationship. The toddler then finds shame an intolerable and overwhelming experience. The process of shame becomes blocked from the child's consciousness. As Alan Shore points out: 'there is an arrest of emotional development'. Hence, a toddler starts to emerge where shame is a psychobiological process that informs the child and develops the interconnectivity of the relationship. It even supports the maturity of the child as an individual. This is why you may have a child in your care who appears to have no shame. A common response is for carers to feel quite angry about this, which is entirely understandable. However, anger just compounds the problem and reminds the child that everyone is always angry with them anyway.

This means that a superhuman effort is needed on the part of the carer to help with this stage of development, which is often damaged in children who are hard to manage. However, you can make progress and again you need to look for the hidden signals. A child will hide mistakes, or you may see a tinge of red in their face at times, or they may get frustrated with themselves. All of these mini signals can be supported by conversations with you, especially when you know what this is all about. It falls down to that idea of interactive repair where the parent helps the child with thoughtful sensitivity to understand the right way to go.

Conclusions on Shame

It is clear that anger is not an option with a child who does not feel shame, although any level of frustration about it is very understandable. Hopefully, more information about why a child in your care does not experience shame is helpful to you.

It is clear that children need interactive support to be able to tolerate the experience of shame. Consequences to actions are a very helpful way to help a child know that what they have done is inappropriate – i.e. having the television taken away for a period because it was broken by thoughtless play. As long as this is done in a sensitive and interactive fashion with an explanation and a conversation, it is helpful to the child. The best possible solutions are gentle explanations that help the child to understand that they have got it wrong, that you are there to help, that you will stay connected and attuned to them, and that you will not abandon them in a rough and dismissive way.

The carer needs to demonstrate 'joined up' thinking in their own mind, showing the child that you can tolerate their mistakes and still care for them. Most children who do not experience shame are often afraid that people will not tolerate them. It is now up to the carer to set the conditions of repair that enable the child to be honest about their experience and make sense of doing wrong.

All of this requires extraordinary tolerance on the part of the carer. The use of empathy and understanding cannot be overestimated as tools to support the child who has probably been inadequately supported in their emotional development. Their shame has never been regulated through interaction with responsible, sensitive others.

Conclusion

In this session we have thought about two conditions that may be fuelling your child's behaviour issues. The first is the way that trauma deeply affects children and makes them appear extremely difficult. The second is the way that lack of parental interaction may have prevented your child from experiencing appropriate shame. They may therefore have no compunction about being harmful and may appear quite arrogant about the things that they do wrong. This is presented to you because trauma and lack of shame are constantly presented to me in my adoption support agency as issues that frequently distress substitute parents and carers. As usual, it is in reflecting more on these issues and increasing your own awareness base that you may be able to make a new plan that can help your child with these conditions.

SESSION NINE
MORE CONDITIONS THAT INFLUENCE BEHAVIOUR

RECIPROCITY

One of the hardest things about looking after a deprived child can be their lack of interaction and joining in with the parent. The role of being a parent is definitely about being in the role of a giver but at the same time in normal situations children give something back in terms of their affectionate interaction and co-operation and responsiveness with the parent. This is known as reciprocity, or being in a reciprocal relationship. Give and take is the basis of any relationship. We all need to be in a reciprocal relationship and it is hard when parents have a sense that the child is taking a lot but giving nothing back. Most of us like to feel a sense of flow in the relationship.

Often this is a consequence of the child's emotional and psychological needs not being met. The main thing to understand about this in order to help is that a child fails to reciprocate because they know of no other experience. I once worked with a child who was quite unkind to others and when I started to talk to him about the experience of being kind, I realised he actually had no idea whatsoever what this experience meant. He had been shown little kindness and was consequently a cruel child. His foster parents mainly had to teach him directly as well as show him from their hearts what kindness meant. While this was an extreme case, there are many children who have an internal sense of people being on the whole mean to them – their inner life is not dominated by kindness and giving. It is perhaps hard to imagine how that might feel.

When children have not received their early care from parents, they have lost a piece of experience that is very important to their development. When a baby is born, the brain is still developing and in fact continues to develop throughout childhood. From the work of neurobiologist Allan Schore we know that the baby's relational and social brain builds first with the frontal lobes and cognitive aspects of brain-development build on the foundation of the social brain in later childhood. This is known as the right brain, which is packed with tiny experiences and stores relational knowledge (all the knowledge we have about relationships). When we talk about the social brain we are talking about the way that the baby relates to people.

Schore refers to this as the 'implicit relational knowledge that is learned before the age of three' Implicit means that it is not conscious to us – it is just stored there. If a child has none of this knowledge encoded into their right brain and there are gaps there we can be sure that the sense of 'reciprocity' or give and take that most of us experience in relationships will be absent. Relationships for such children are not about give and take, enjoyment and empathy – they are just about staying safe, being ready to identify threat and getting all that is needed to survive. So the children in our care are going to be ready to identify threat and react as a main priority in order to stay safe effectively. They do not turn to relationships in order to stay safe. Their brain is so involved with survival that they are not released even to enjoy relationships.

This is why the children in our care who are difficult to care for and who do not form relationships easily frequently come across as hard work and unrewarding. Consequently, they don't get the help that they need from people. Carers become exasperated and exhausted, and may actually withdraw because it appears that the child actually prefers to live in a world of their own. It could be very easy not to bother with these children and to leave them in their own world.

The question is, then, when and how to connect to a child who has no sense that relationships with others can be deeply rewarding and help them to feel relaxed, happy and confident as well as being able to give something back to the relationship.

The answer is that we should not force this issue as it simply forms a kind of 'combat' with the child whereby they resist attention that is being forced on them. It simply ends in a fight or the child putting up even more of a false self in order to cope. There are behaviours that we can demonstrate that increase the child's sense of connectedness and reliance on others over time. Here are some ideas for you.

Where to start to help your child with Reciprocity

- Back to alliance building. Make explicit the ground rules for safety within the context of your home and child's life with you. Do this from the very beginning. 'We want you to feel safe in this house and so ...'. This is part of the alliance building we have already talked about.

- Begin the relationship with safety in mind as this child is watching out for the mistakes that they are sure you will make to let them down.

- Be prepared to make everything you do explicit. This may be tedious but at least the child realises that what you say you are going to do and what you do are the same thing. 'I am just going out to get the washing in' implies that you are not disappearing and leaving the child. 'We are going to put the TV on at 6 p.m. –there's a really funny programme on' implies that you are not switching off and ignoring the child. 'We get up early but you don't have to get up until later 'implies' that you are not walking around making plans to hurt you or to leave the child.

- Keep joining up events for this child in a soft and gentle way. Keep much information about your actions available and explicit.

- Engage in as much interactivity as possible in daily life rather than letting the child exist in a world of their own – i.e. talking about what you are cooking and getting the child to help you lay the table. With small children this means playing games.

- Play as many games as you can that involve interactivity. Avoid excessive games that are about the child sitting on their own for hours at a time.

- Demonstrate interactivity with others. Let the child watch you interacting with others in a reciprocal way. Be explicit about interacting.

- You could run through the plan for the day with the child. If you make changes, explain why. If you show the child that they are connected to you, you are interacting with them.

- Every infant craves and desires the attention of their parent. The goal is to encourage children to enjoy the safety and fun of your attention.

- If you have an older child and they spring surprises on you with their own unpredictable behaviour, there may appear to be no joined-up thinking in the things that they do due to the lack of reciprocity. Try to help them join that thinking and behaviour.

- The child may not know what to do to contribute to the relationship. You may have to instruct them and get them to help you in small ways so that they learn that contributing is a positive experience.

TIME TO THINK ABOUT RECIPROCITY

Write a list of ten experiences that will assist positive interactions and start to build tolerance of positive effects for your child, beginning with small experiences every day that can be sustained by you and that can be incorporated with regularity. Here are some of the ideas that I have used:

Teatime – always at 4.00 p.m. (but you could have night-time drinks time). A special time to relax together.

A weekly comic that you work on together.

Who gets to chose the menu for dinner today?

Card making – something to do for others but fun craft together.

Colouring in together. Brilliant for adults as you don't have to think too much about this.

Developmental Delay

As a result of trauma, repressed shame and lack of reciprocity, it is highly likely that a badly treated child may be delayed in their development. It is often easy for development to be uneven so that a child who appears to be coping at an age-appropriate level at school may have the emotional age that is years younger because of neglect and lack of attention to their emotional life. Parents and carers can be baffled by the apparent regression. It can be mystifying and frustrating.

The piece to understand about this is that it is happening – it is not your imagination. The more loving attention we can give to a child's regressed state, the more likely they are to move on from that state. Again, it is a matter of management. You are not going to encourage your ten-year-old to play with playdough when they are going out of the door for school. However, it could be something you do on a Saturday morning as a regular ritual which gives acknowledgement to that child. Nurturing for a teenager is hardly going to involve sitting on your lap in front of the television, but it could involve a special bedtime drink made with loving care and attention, lots of positive hugs, smiles and kindly looks, and a sensitive tone of voice – and attention to detail. You could serve nursery food to a teenager – feeding the tiny neglected infant inside them while at the same time allowing them time for their normal teenage ego development.

Children will give confusing messages about travelling backwards developmentally, which can be quite baffling at times. They will try to stop the tendency to regress because they feel it does not fit in with the everyday pattern of life, but then they will demonstrate desperately needy behaviours and want the smallest things from you in order to gain your loving attention.

The thing to hold on to is that regression is not mad or crazy. People sometimes see this as wrong or weird. Regression is a perfectly healthy response to a difficult situation. The everyday mind closes down for a while and that repressed part of the self that has been dying for attention emerges. We can all do that. Take, for example, when you feel ill or have the flu. What do you feel like? You want your mum to look after you. Take a very healthy child aged ten who goes down with flu. They completely dissolve into the helplessness of a small child until the minute they are feeling better, at which point they regain their mental resources and off they go to get on with ordinary life. It may take a little longer with a child who is chronically neglected. It may take years instead of months, but be friends with this tendency and your child will soon be able to integrate that forgotten aspect of themselves into their personality. You will also be giving them something wonderful by showing that you care and that you understand how very difficult life is for them internally. A few hours of playdough on a Saturday with your ten-year-old could make all the difference to them. Recently I have taken to making my own playdough – adding essential oils of lavender and rose. This means that a bit of squidgy play also becomes an opportunity for soothing and relaxation.

I am including some charts on development that are a mixture of the work of Alan Sroufe (2004) on child development and the work of Vera Fahlberg (1991) These may help you to identify the stage that your child is trying to demonstrate through their behaviour.

Developmental Delay

Babies: birth–12 months – normal development

- Infant is totally dependent.

- Development in the first year of life is set towards the goal of attachment in the care-giver. Baby cries when upset and needs comfort, but learns to engage others through smiling.

- During this period sensitive care is crucial.

- Interaction, talking and play with the baby help the developing brain.

- The infant brain is dependent on relationship and interactivity in order to promote brain development.

- Brain development in the first year is oriented towards relationship and learning with others.

- Parent provides routine – baby enjoys this.

- Baby shows excitement when kicking arms and legs.

- Baby loves to look at people and gaze, and loves it when people gaze back.

- Baby has emotions soothed by caring adults.

These lists are a combination of the work on attachment and child development of Vera Fahlberg to be found in 'A Child's Journey Through Placement (1991) Published by BAAF (British Association of Adoption and Fostering) and Child Development Its Nature and Course 5th Edition (2004) By Ganie B.DeHart, L.Alan Sroufe and Robert G . Cooper

Toddlers: 12-30 months – normal develpoment

- Child becomes aware of preferred attachment figure and can be clingy.

- Parents support and increase tendency to explore the world and provide a safe environment. They also set limits for the child.

- The toddler still enjoys routine which parents need to provide.

- Parents talk frequently to their child who in turn is learning to chatter to them. By 18 months the child can say a few words. Interaction is still key to development.

- Parents help the child to become more aware of others. The child begins to learn that others have intentions as well.

- Parents help the toddler with increased sociability. Expectations must be realistic so that the child is confident about social interactions.

- The toddler shows a wider range of emotional response, including tantrums and rage. The child can express happy, mad and sad. Parents support this development in a kindly way that is not destructive and that helps the child to manage these overwhelming emotions.

- Parents help the child to internalise rules and the child begins to show self-control.

🐬 By 24 months the child starts to use words to communicate if parents chat to child consistently but not in baby talk.

These lists are a combination of the work on attachment and child development of Vera Fahlberg to be found in 'A Child's Journey Through Placement (1991) Published by BAAF (British Association of Adoption and Fostering) and Child Development Its Nature and Course 5th Edition (2004) By Ganie B.DeHart, L.Alan Sroufe and Robert G . Cooper

Pre-chooler (adapted from Clausen, 1968 in Sroufe, 2004): 2½–5 years – normal development

🐬 Enjoys books and games. Can play independently.

🐬 Child still highly dependent on adult support and responsiveness.

🐬 Can now separate from care-giver more easily in familiar places but not in strange places.

🐬 Parents need to offer nurturing and children need to be able to accept care and develop their trust in their carers and other adults.

🐬 Parents need to train their children and help them with their physical activities. Children in turn will comply with parental intervention and learn to control themselves.

🐬 Parents will orientate the child to their family and to peers in the outside world. The child will develop a general understanding of the outside world.

🐬 Parents will promote interpersonal skills and control of emotions at appropriate times. Children of this age will engage in playing roles.

🐬 Parents will help with control of emotion and children will be achieving their self-regulation.

🐬 Parents will transmitt their values and the child will learn right from wrong. The child can follow simple directions, and understands and responds to the word 'no'.

Children of this age begin to show feeling for others and to notice other people's feelings and understand that others have intentions. Parents listen and respond to the toddler's spoken and expressed feelings. Parents continue to offering special comfort and nurturing.

These lists are a combination of the work on attachment and child development of Vera Fahlberg to be found in 'A Child's Journey Through Placement (1991) Published by BAAF (British Association of Adoption and Fostering) and Child Development Its Nature and Course 5th Edition (2004) By Ganie B.DeHart, L.Alan Sroufe and Robert G . Cooper

Middle childhood: 6–12 years – normal development

- Needs prompts with remembering but better attention and memory.

- Needs parental support with learning and emotions but may turn to friends for help. Can undertake self-care but needs parental reminders and support.

- There are strict rules to gender contact, and boys and girls of this age tend to mix less at school and have a code of practice. There is a desire to conform.

- Children start to form a coherent sense of themselves. They can talk about their inner life as well as their thoughts and feelings. They can talk about a psychological self – they have a mind.

- There is an emphasis on peer relations.

- There is an emerging capability to manage emotions separately from the main attachment figure. Middle years' children can make more sense of their emotions. They show more empathy for others and show that they understand there are rules to relating.

These lists are a combination of the work on attachment and child development of Vera Fahlberg to be found in 'A Child's Journey Through Placement (1991) Published by BAAF (British Association of Adoption and Fostering) and Child Development Its Nature and Course 5th Edition (2004) By Ganie B.DeHart, L.Alan Sroufe and Robert G . Cooper

Teenager: 12–18 years – normal development

- There is a transformation of physical appearance.

- There is an increase in egocentrism.

- Starts to establish identity: 'who will I be?'

- Peer relations are a major source of personal development.

- There will be drastic changes in patterns of interaction within the family.

- There is a push for autonomy and independence. Parents may feel rejected.

- Child relationships have to realign themselves and this is often characterised by conflict.

- Warm authoritative parenting continues to be the most supportive type of parenting as opposed to authoritarian or passive parenting.

These lists are a combination of the work on attachment and child development of Vera Fahlberg to be found in 'A Child's Journey Through Placement (1991) Published by BAAF (British Association of Adoption and Fostering) and Child Development Its Nature and Course 5th Edition (2004) By Ganie B.DeHart, L.Alan Sroufe and Robert G . Cooper

TRAINING TASKS TO HELP YOU TO THINK ON DEVELOPMENTAL DELAY AND RECIPROCITY

1   Think of a time when you were really ill, had a nasty shock or felt really upset about some event in your life. What were your needs at this time and what did you need from people to support you? Did you feel and think like an adult when you were most upset?

2   If you were given a chance to have a day of having your needs totally met and you did not have to feel responsible for anything, what would that day look like? Few people have this opportunity, but at least we can think about the freedom of having our needs met and maybe every now and then we can have a day just for ourselves so that we experience a sense of being cared for – just as we are having to care all the time. This is about being able to imagine that you could let go and be cared for. This is the experience that we want the children in our care to have. We need them to 'let go' and trust in adult care.

To give you an idea, my day would look like this:

Breakfast in bed – cooked breakfast, not toast

Lie in bed and listen to radio all morning.

Go back to sleep for short rest after taxing morning.

Go to spa in the afternoon for facial and manicure and chat with girlfriends.

Go out for afternoon tea to include scones and cream with the same girlfriends.

Short lie down to recover from afternoon exertions while listening to a play on the   radio.

Get changed into beautiful going-out clothes.

Go out for dinner.

Conclusion

In this session we looked at the experience of children needing to regress or go backwards to earlier years in their behaviour. I encouraged the view that if we are supportive and not afraid of this that we can really help children to move forwards. Often parents are afraid that if they support children who are displaying behaviour of a much younger child that they will not help them to develop. Sometimes children go backwards because they really need to. In addition we explored the reasons for children not being able to give anything back to their new parents. This is often referred to as reciprocity but simply put it means the give and take or flow of relationships. Children who have not been helped with interactive parents are often uncooperative and appear to live in a world of their own. We looked at how to encourage this interactivity. We also looked at allowing yourself to let go and enjoy a sense of being supported and I have encouraged you to have days when you are totally supported and nurtured. You wont be able to do this every day but just once in a while will teach you to remember what it is like to be a supported child. You need this luxury every once in a while.

SESSION TEN

CONCLUSION
PREPARING YOUR NERVOUS SYSTEM TO COPE
MANTRAS FOR MAINTAINING MINDFULNESS

We are coming to the end of this opportunity to reflect together on your experience with your child. You have covered a lot of ground in understanding yourself and the child in your care. You may feel stretched by this emotionally and mentally. If you do, it is fine to put the book down and let your system settle. No doubt you can come back to any issues that arise for you when you are ready. You should feel that you can take the time to consider issues in a time frame to suit you – that is the nature of psychological development and change. It takes time – your time. The key thesis of this reader and workbook is that you are likely to have to adapt and change in order to support the child in your care. Sometimes this can be a baffling and bewildering experience and you need good support.

Another concept that I have tried to put forward is that it is always the carer's/parent's state of mind that is the relevant issue. How the provider of the secure base continues to bring that support forward for their child is what matters. Often very troubled children can disturb the equilibrium of their new attachment figures, meaning that for a while everyone lives in chaos. Disturbed and troubled children will continue to be disturbed and troubled and present challenging behaviour, until they fully experience a secure base of care where they can rely on thoughtful and mindful adults.

This workbook encourages you to be aware of your own state of mind so that you are in control of your own responses to your child. One way to achieve this is by being aware of the thoughts that go through your mind about your experience at any one given moment in time. The way that you think about a situation is entirely a matter of your own self-management. You can regulate your emotions by managing the thoughts that go through your head and ensuring that you have the correct information about your child. This is the formula: 'What am I thinking about this?'

To help you, here are some thoughts that you can have about your situation. You could let these thoughts or mantras run your mind. A parent who helped me with the research for this workbook had her own mantra that she found in a child's story book. It went like this: 'Can't go round it, can't go over it, got to go through it.' She reminded herself of this when she had to deal with her child's catastrophic states of relentless anxiety. It helped to remind her of the best direction and to focus her thoughts. She understood that her child could not help this behaviour and that the only way to help it to change was to listen intently to the messages of the child's emotional state. After two years of very hard work, that mother found that she was able to offer a secure base on which this child could make changes and develop into a much happier child. There was no quick fix.

Here are the same mindful messages for you to choose and use to support your journey.

Messages to keep you mindful

You are not to blame for the child's behavioural disturbance, but the solution to the problem lies in the quality of parenting that the child receives from you now.

On days when you don't feel very good about the relationship with this child, you could remember that you can form an alliance in which you only have to help the child to feel safe. If you concentrate on this task you might not worry so much about the state of the relationship, which will gradually evolve from a place of safety.

This child behaves in this way because they are afraid of relationships with adults, not because they hate you.

You can choose which role to play in this relationship. Some days you may be expected to play the 'bad guy' but you don't have to do that if you don't want to.

You cannot always help the child in your care by giving them lots of material objects. It is quite possible that excessive fun, joy and activity may be too much and may get in the way of the child's recovery. Less is more in this case.

You don't have to go to Alton Towers to make this child happy. In fact, it doesn't make other kids happy. What makes children happy is a safe, secure, predictable relationship with an adult. You could stay home, miss the traffic and have fun in the garden.

You don't have to be rich, well educated or dressed in designer clothes to help this child recover. You do have to be calm, peaceful, well balanced and receptive.

The most precious thing that you can demonstrate to the child in your care is that you can manage your own state of mind, and that you can therefore help them to manage theirs too.

You have a choice about how you respond in any given situation. The child in your care probably has not. If things are getting heated, you can step to one side for as long as it takes to feel better and find a good resolution.

Lower the barrier if your child is resistant to you. Never be afraid to back down if that is what it takes for a peaceful solution. If backing down helps a distressed situation to de-escalate, then do it . You can deal with regaining your control later by discussing the situation with a calm child.

Don't try to make sense of things with a distressed child. They cannot do it then. When children are distressed offer soothing, in any suitable form. Discussion comes later when they feel better.

If you work hard at anything, make sure it is the very thing that will give you the most results – the child's emotional life. The key to this is listening, understanding and reflection.

Never undervalue the centrality of emotions to our well being and balanced mental health. Value the emotions of others and your own emotions. Never be too proud to ask for support.

Managing a child's emotional life with them and for them is the new designer label – have you got yours?

Check your automatic thinking. What you think is what you get. It really is OK to be honest with yourself about how you are thinking and far more productive.

All of this cannot be resolved today. Repairing the mind and behaviour of a broken child takes months and years, not days and weeks. You don't have to fix this all now.

You can chase a child around the drama triangle all day or the child can chase you. You can adopt a role that you don't want to play, or you can just be mindful of what is happening now for this child. It is probably not about you.

You are a great parent because you are doing all you can to help this child to rediscover that relationships can be helpful and safe. You deserve all the support you can get.

Never be too afraid to ask for help or share your thoughts and feelings with someone who genuinely feels for you and supports you.

The look on your face and tone of your voice will say 80 per cent of what you really mean. Model as much kind thoughtfulness as you possibly can for the child in your care.

Always repair rifts in the relationship with your child. You are only human and you are allowed to get angry. Being really human is about repairing relationships in a kind and loving way.

It is very unlikely that your child is behaving badly on purpose. They don't have a choice about how they behave until they are better – do you?

A child's behaviour changes within the context of loving and interactive relationships – it rarely changes with a good telling off. If a telling off really is the answer, don't forget to make good repair when you are ready.

As far as is possible and sensible, offer explanations and joined-up thinking to the child in your care about everything that happens in their lives – even the small things. This will help them to know that you are thinking about them.

A child who is low on empathy for others has probably never received enough empathy. How many opportunities can you find for empathic responses today?

Are you having some fun, or is this task making you miserable? Whereas the child in your care is relying on you to increase their capacity to cope with happiness, the hard truth is that the only person responsible for your happiness is you.

Thoughts can change, feelings can change, behaviour can change and people can change. Positive changes are a likely outcome of a secure base for a child.

Flight Captain Sullenberger landed his plane in the Hudson River and saved all his passengers because he stayed in control of his emotions (January 2009). Can you land that plane in the Hudson today?

Every time you remain in control of your fight of flight responses you teach your child something miraculous about life – and you are the hero.

Wishing you well for your journey.

Joanna North

Bibliography

Ainsworth, M.D.S. (1967) *Infancy in Uganda: Infant Care and the Growth of Love*, Baltimore, MD: The Johns Hopkins University Press.

Ainsworth, M.D.S. (1982) 'Attachment: Retrospect and Prospect', in C.M. Parkes and J. Stevenson-Hinde (eds) *The Place of Attachment in Human Behaviour*, New York: Basic Books, pp. 3–30.

Ainsworth, M.D.S., Blehar, M.C., Waters, E. and Wall, S. (1978) *Patterns of Attachment: A Psychological Study of the Strange Situation*, Hillsdale, NJ: Erlbaum.

Alvarez, A. (1992) *Live Company: Psychoanalytic Psychotherapy with Autistic, Borderline, Deprived and Abused Children*, London and New York: Routledge.

Alveson, M. and Skoldberg, K. (2000) *New Vistas for Qualitative Research*, London: Sage.

American Psychiatric Association (2000) (4th edn) *DSM IV: Diagnostic and Statistical Manual of Mental Disorders*, Arlington, VA: American Psychiatric Association.

Antrichan, J. (Chair of UKCP) (2007) 'Foreword', in P. Jenkin, *Counselling Psychotherapy and The Law*, London: Sage.

Archer, C. and Burnell, A. (2003) *Trauma, Attachment and Family Permanence: Fear Can Stop you Loving*, London: Jessica Kingsley Publishing.

Axeline, V. (1990) *Dibs in Search of Self*, London: Random House Publishing.

Bleiberg, E. (2004) *Treating Personality Disorders in Children and Adolescents: A Relational Approach*, New York: Guilford Press.

Boris N., Hinshaw-Fuselier, S., Smyke, A., Scheeringa, M., Heller, S. and Zeanah, C. (2004) 'Comparing criteria for attachment disorders: establishing reliability and validity in high risk samples', *Journal of the American Academy of Child and Adolescent Psychiatry*, 43: 568-77, reprinted in V. Prior, V. and Glaser, D. (2006) *Understanding Attachment and Attachment Disorders*, London: Jessica Kingsley, p. 250.

Bowlby, J. (1944) 'Fortyfour juvenile theives, their characters and home lives' *International Journal of Psycho-Analysis*, 25: 19–53.

Bowlby, J. (1953) *Childcare and the Growth of Love*, London: Penguin.

Bowlby, J. (1969) *Attachment and Loss, Vol. 1, Attachment*, London: Pimlico / Random House Publishing.

Bowlby, J. (1973) *Attachment and Loss, Vol. 2, Separation: Anxiety and Anger*, NewYork: Basic Books.

Bowlby, J. (1981) *Attachment and Loss, Vol. 3, Loss, Sadness and Depression*, New York: Basic Books.

Bowlby, J. ([1979] 1989) *The Making and Breaking of Affectional Bonds*, originally published by Tavistock Publications, London: Routledge.

Bowlby, J. (1988) *A Secure Base*, London: Routledge.

Bowlby, J. (1990) *Charles Darwin: A New Life*, New York: Norton.

Bowlby, R. (2007) 'Babies and toddlers in non-parental day care can avoid stress and anxiety if they develop a lasting secondary attachment bond with one carer', *Attachment & Human Development*, December, 9(4): 303–8.

Bowlby, R. (2007) 'Keep on pushing: an interview with Richard Bowlby', *Attachment: New Directions in Psychotherapy and Relational Psychoanalysis*, 1: 62–4, March.

British Association of Counselling and Psychotherapy (2009) (revised edn) Lutterworth.

Campbell, D.T. and Stanley, J.C. (1966) *Experimental and Quasi-Experimental Designs for Research*, Chicago: Rand McNally.

Chamberlain, P. (1998) *Family Connections: A Treatment Foster Care Model for Adolescents with Delinquency*, Eugene, OR: Castalia Publishing.

Cohen, N.J., Muire, E., Lojkasek, M., Muire, R., Parker, C.J., Barwick, M. and Brown, M. (1999) 'Watch, wait and wonder: testing the effectiveness of a new approach to mother infant psychotherapy', *Infant Mental Health Journal*, 20(4): 429–51.

Costley, C. and Portwood, D. (2000) *Work Based Learning and the University: New Perpective and Practices*, Birmingham: SEDA.

Courtois, C.A. (1977) 'Healing the incest wound: a treatment update with attention to the recovered memory issue', *American Journal of Psychotherapy*, 51: 464–96. In

Textbook of Psychotherapy, Oxford University Press 2005 - Holmes, J., Gabbard, O., Beck, B. and Judith, S.

Darwin, C. (1928) *The Origin of Species by Means of Natural Selection,* London: J.M. Dent.

Denzin, K. and Lincoln, Y.S. (2005) (3rd edn) 'Preface' in *The SAGE Handbook of Qualitative Research,* London: Sage.

Ellis, A. and Harper, R.A. (1975) *A New Guide to Rational Living,* Englewood Cliffs, NJ: Prentice-Hall.

Etherington, K. (2004) *Becoming a Reflexive Researcher: Using Our Selves in Research,* Chapter 7, 'Reflexive Interpretations', London: Jessica Kingsley Publishing.

Fishman, D.B. (1999) *The Case for a Pragmatic Psychology,* New York: New York University Press.

Flyvbjerg, B. (2006) 'Five misunderstandings about case study research', *Qualitative Inquiry,* 12(2): 219–45, April.

Fonagy, P. and Target, M. (1997) 'Attachment and reflective function: their role in self-organisation', *Development and Psychopathology,* 9, 679–700.

Fonagy, P., Gergely, G., Jurist, E. and Target, M. (2004) *Affect Regulation, Mentalization and the Development of the Self,* London: Karnac.

Fontana, A. and Frey, J. (2000) In Kim Etherington's study 'Heuristic research as a vehicle for personal and professional development', *Counselling and Psychotherapy Research* (2004), 4 (2), (p. 62).

Ford, G. (1997) *The Contented Little Baby Book,* Fontana, CA: Fontana.

Foucault, M. (1966) *Les Mots et les choses,* trans. *The Order of Things* (1970), London: Tavistock Publications; (1989) London: Routledge.

George, C., Kaplan, N. and Main, M. (1984, 1985, 1996) 'Adult Attachment Interview Protocol', Department of Psychology, University of California at Berkeley. Copyright Regents of the University of California, 2002.

Gerhardt, S. (2004) *Why Love Matters: How Affection Shapes a Baby's Brain,* New York: Brunner-Routledge.

Gilbert, P. (1989) *Human Nature and Suffering,* London: LEA.

Goleman, D. (1996) *Emotional Intelligence,* London: Bloomsbury.

Hamilton, V. (2007) 'The nature of a student's tie to the teacher: reminiscences of training and friendship with John Bowlby', *Attachment: New Directions in Psychotherapy and Relational Psychoanalysis*, 1(3): 341, November.

Harlow, H.F. (1962) 'The development of affectional patterns in infant monkeys', in B.M. Foss (ed.) *Determinants of Infant Behaviour, Vol. 1*, New York: Wiley, pp. 75–88.

Hinde, R. (2007) Interview with F. van der Horst at St John's College, Cambridge, *Attachment & Human Development*, 9 (4): 321–35, December.

Hodges, J., Steele, M., Hillman, S., Henderson, K. and Kaniuk, J. (2003) 'Changes in attachment representations over the first year of adoptive placement: narratives of maltreated children', *Clinical Child Psychology and Psychiatry*, 8, 351–67.

Holmes, J. (1993) *John Bowlby and Attachment Theory*, London: Routledge.

Holmes, J. (2005) *The Search for the Secure Base: Attachment Theory and Psychotherapy*, London: Routledge.

Holmes, J. (2007) 'Sex, couples, and attachment: the role of hedonic intersubjectivity', *Attachment: New Directions in Psychotherapy and Relational Psychoanalysis*, 1:18–29, March.

Holmes, J., Kraemer, S. and Steele, H. (2007) 'A tribute to the legacy of John Bowlby at the centenary of his birth', *Attachment & Human Development*, 9(4): 303–6, December.

Horrocks, C. and Jevtic, Z. (1997) *Foucault for Beginners*, London: Icon Books.

Howe, D. (2003) 'Attachment disorders: disinhibited attachment behaviours and secure base distortions with special reference to adopted children', *Attachment & Human Development* , 5(3): 265–270, September.

Howe, D. (2005) *Child Abuse and Neglect: Attachment, Development and Intervention*, Basingstoke: Palgrave Macmillan.

Howe, D., Brandon, M., Hinings, D. and Schofield, G. (1999) *Attachment Theory, Child Maltreatment and Family Support: A Practice and Assessment Model*, Basingstoke: Palgrave Macmillan.

Hughes, D.A. (2006) *Building the Bonds of Attachment: Awakening Love in Deeply Troubled Children*, New York: Jason Aronson.

International Society for the Study of Dissociation (2000) 'Guidelines for treating dissociative identity disorders (multiple personality) in adults' (1970), *Journal of Trauma and Dissociation* 2, 117–34.

Kennerley, H. (1996) 'Cognitive therapy of dissociative symptoms associated with trauma', *British Journal of Clinical Psychology*, 35: 325–40.

Kraemer, S., Steele, H. and Holmes, J. (2007) 'A tribute to the legacy of John Bowlby at the centenary of his birth', *Attachment & Human Development*, 9(4): 303, December.

Levy, T. (1999) *Handbook of Attachment Interventions*, San Diego, CA: Academic Press.

Lieberman, A. F. (2003) 'The treatment of attachment disorder in infancy and early childhood: reflections from clinical intervention with later adopted foster care children', *Attachment & Human Development*, 5(3): 279–82, September.

Liotti, G. (1999) 'Disorganised attachment as a model for the understanding of dissociative psychopathology', in J. Solomon and C. George (eds) *Attachment Disorganisation*, New York: Guilford Press, pp. 291–317.

Liotti, G., Mollon, P. and Miti, G. (2007) 'Dissociative Disorders' in G.O. Gabbard, J.S. Beck and J. Holmes (eds) *Oxford Textbook of Psychotherapy*, Oxford and New York: Oxford University Press, pp. 203–11.

Lyons-Ruth, K., Melnick, S., Patrick, M. and Hobson, R.P. (2007) 'A controlled study of Hostile-Helpless states of mind among borderline and dysthymic women', *Attachment & Human Development*, 9(1), March.

Madigan S, Bakermans Kranenburg M. J., Van Ijzendoorn M.H., Moran G, Pederson D. and Benoit D. (2006) *Unresolved states of mind, anomalous parental behaviour, and disorganised attachment: a review and meta analysis of a transmission gap.* Attachment and Human Development June 2006; 8(2): 89–111. Routledge Taylor and Francis

Magagna, J. (2003) 'Clinical concepts and caregiving contexts: a consultant's perspective', in C. Archer and A. Burnell (eds) *Trauma, Attachment and Family Permanence: Fear Can Stop You Loving*, London: Jessica Kingsley, pp. 99–113.

Main, M. (1999) 'Epilogue: Eighteen points with suggestions for further study' (point thirteen), in J. Cassidy and P.R. Shaver (eds) *The Handbook of Attachment: Theory, Research and Clinical Applications,* New York: Guilford Press, pp. 845–7.

Main, M. and Goldwyn, R. (1984) 'Adult attachment scoring and classification system', unpublished manuscript, Berkeley, CA: University of California.

Main, M. and Solomon, J. (1990) 'Procedures for identifying infants as disorganised during the Ainsworth Strange Situation', in M.T. Greenberg, D. Cicchetti and E.M. Cummings (eds) *Attachment in the Preschool Years: Theory, Research, and Intervention*, Chicago: University of Chicago Press, pp. 121–60.

Marvin, R., Cooper, G., Hoffman, K. and Powell, B. (2002) 'The circle of security project: attachment base intervention with caregiver in pre-school child dyads', *Attachment & Human Development*, 4(1): 107–24, April.

McLeod, J. (1994) *Doing Counselling Research*, London: Sage, Chapter 7.

McLeod, J. (2009) 'Writing a practice-based case study for publication', Information sheet written for the BACP, Tayside Institute for Health Studies, University of Abertay, Dundee.

McLeod, J. (2009) 'Notes and Overheads' at a lecture at the Metanoia Institute as part of the Professional Knowledge Seminars, 6 July, The Metanoia Institute, Ealing, London.

Mercer, J., Sarner, L. and Rosa, L. (2003) *Attachment Therapy on Trial: The Torture and Death of Candace*, Westport, CT: Praeger.

Miller, R.B. (2004) *Facing Human Suffering: Psychology and Psychotherapy as Moral Engagement*, Washington, DC: American Psychological Association.

Muir, R. (undated) Speaking on Transgenerational Transmission, The Hinks Centre, in an interview with Richard Bowlby.

National Research Council of America (2005) in K. Denzin and Y.S. Lincoln (eds)

Denzin, Norman K. and Lincoln, Yvonna S. (2000) "The Discipline and Practice of Qualitative Research", in *The SageHandbook of Qualitative Research,* 3rd edn, London: Sage, p. 8.

North, J. (2004) 'Factors that Affect the Successful Fostering of Children with Difficult Behaviour', MA thesis, Bath: University of Bath Spa College.

North, J. (2008) 'Attachment: new directions', in *Psychotherapy and Relational Psychoanalysis*, 2(1).

Oakley A. (1981) *Subject Women*, Oxford: Martin Robertson.

O'Connor, T. and Zeanah, C. (2003) 'Current perspectives on assessment and treatment of attachment disorders', *Attachment and Human Development* (special issue), 5(3), September.

Olesen, V. (2005) 'Early millennial feminist qualitive research: challenges and contours', in N.K. Denzin and Y.S. Lincoln (eds) *The Sage Handbook of Qualitative Research* (3rd edn), Thousand Oaks, CA: Sage.

Pasquini, P., Liotti, G. and the Italian Group for the Study of Dissociation (2002) 'Risk factors in the early family life of patients suffering from dissociative disorders, *Acta Psychiatrica Scandinanvica*, 105, pp. 110–16.

Piaget, J. (1929) *The Child's Conception of the World*, New York: Harcourt-Brace.

Powell T. (2009) *The Mental Health Handbook. A Cognitive Behavioural Approach.* 3rd Edition. Speechmarks Publishing

Quinodoz, Jean-Michel (2008) 'Beyond the pleasure principle', in *Reading Freud: A Chronological Exploration of Freud's Writings*, New York: Routledge.

Schore, A.N. (1994) *Affect Regulation and the Origin of the Self: The Neurobiology of Emotional Development*, Hillsdale, NJ: Lawrence Erlbaum Publishers.

Shapiro, E. (2001) (2nd edn) *Eye Movement Desensitizaton and Reprocessing: Basic Principles, Protocols and Procedures*, New York: Guilford Press.

Slade, A. (1999) 'Attachment theory and research implications for the theory and practice of individual psychotherapy with adults', in J. Cassidy and P. Shaver (eds) *The Handbook of Attachment Theory*, New York: Guilford Press.

Slade, A. (2005) 'Parental reflective functioning', *Attachment and Human Development*, 7(3): 269–81, September.

Slade, A. (2008) 'The move from categories and process: attatchment phenomenon and (clinical) evauluation', *Attachment: New Directions in Psychotherapy and Relational Psychoanalysis*, 2(1).

Spock, B. (1966) *Baby and Child Care*, London: Bodley Head.

Sroufe, L.A. (2005) 'Attachment and development: a prospective, longitudinal study from birth to adulthood', *Attachment and Human Development*, 7(4): 349–68.

Sroufe, L.A., DeHart, G.B. and Cooper, R.G. (2005) (5th edn) *Child Development: its Nature and Course*, London: McGraw Hill.

Sroufe, A., Egeland, B., Carlson, E. and Collins, W.A. (2005) *The Development of the Person: The Minnesota Study of Risk and Adaptation from Birth to Adulthood*, New York: Guilford Press.

Stake, E. (2005) 'Qualitative case studies' in N. Denzin and Y. Lincoln (eds), *The Sage Handbook of Qualitative Research*, Thousand Oaks, CA: Sage, p. 443.

Steele, H. (2003) 'Holding therapy is not attachment therapy', Editor's introduction, *Attachment and Human Development*, special edition, 5(3).

Steele, H. (2003) "Current perspectives on assessment and treatment of attachment disorders", T. O'Connor and C. Zeanah (eds), *Attachment and Human Development*, special issue, 5(3), September.

Steele, M., Hodges, J., Kaniuk, J., Hillman, S. and Henderson, K. (2003) 'Attachment representations and adoption: associations between maternal states of mind and emotion narratives in previously maltreated children', *Journal of Child Psychotherapy*, 29, 187–205.

Stern, D.N. (1995) *The Motherhood Constellation: A Unified View of Parent Infant Psychotherapy*, New York: Basic Books.

Stern, D.N. (1998) *The Interpersonal World of the Infant: A View from Psychoanalysis and Developmental Psychology*, London: Karnac.

Stern, D.N. (2004) *The Present Moment in Psychotherapy and Everyday Life*, New York: Norton.

Tronick, E.Z. (1989) 'Emotions and emotional communication in infants', *American Psychologist*, 44: 112–19.

van der Kolk, B. (1994) 'The body keeps the score: memory and the evolving psychobiology of posttraumatic stress', *Harvard Review of Psychiatry*, 1(5), 253–65.

van der Kolk, B., McFarlane, A., Weisaeth L. (1996) *Traumatic Stress: The Effects of Overwhelming Experience on Mind, Body and Society*, New York: Guilford Press.

van Ijzendoorn, M.H. and Bakermans-Kranenburg, M.J. (1996) 'Attachment representations in mothers fathers and adolescents.' in Journal of Consulting and clinical Psychology 64: 8–21 in Howe D. (1999) *Attachment Theory, Child Maltreatment and Family Support*, London: Palgrave, p. 39.

Williams, R. (Archbishop of Canterbury) (2009) *The Times*, p. 19, 2 February.

Winnicot, D. (1977) *The Piggle: An Account of the Psychoanalytic Treatment of a Little Girl*, Harmondsworth: Penguin.

World Health Organization (1992) 'Classification of mental and behavioural disorders' in the *International Statistical Classification of Diseases and Related Health Problems* (10th edn), Geneva: WHO.

Films

Attenborough, D. (2009) *Darwin*, Sunday, 1 February, 9 pm, BBC One.

Schore, A.M. (1996) Interviewed by Richard Bowlby in his home-made video, *Attachment and Child Development*. Available only from Richard Bowlby at Wyldes Close, London NW11 7JB. Send video and postage on request.